THE P⊙SSIBILITY

My More than Forty-Year Journey to Try to Become a Scratch Golfer

GREG THIESEN

CONTENTS

FOREWORD

GOLF IS A GAME. IT IS EASY TO FORGET THAT IT IS JUST A GAME. NEVER FORGET WHY YOU PLAY.

The following letter is from *Extraordinary Golf* by Fred Shoemaker

"Dear Younger Me:

I cannot play golf anymore. I tried to swing the club the other day, but my body would not cooperate. The best I can do now is sometimes take walks on the course, but my eyes are not as good as they used to be so I do not see much. I have a lot of time to sit and think now, and I often think about the game.

It was my favorite game. I played most of my adult life. Thousands of rounds, thousands of hours practicing. As I look back, I guess I had a pretty good time at it. But now that I can't do it anymore, I wish I had done it differently.

It's funny, but with all the time I spent playing golf, I never thought I was a real golfer. I never felt good enough to really belong out there. It does not make much sense, since I scored better than average and a lot of people envied my game, but I always felt that if I was just a little better or a little more consistent, then I would feel good. I'd be satisfied with my game. But I never was. It was always *One of these days I'll get it* or *One day I'll get there* and now here I am. I can't play anymore, and I never got there.

I met a whole lot of different people out on the course. That was one of the best things about the game. But aside from my regular partners and a few others, I don't feel like I got to know many of those people very well. I know they didn't really get to know me. At times they didn't want to. I was occupied with my own game most of the time, and didn't have much time for anyone else, especially if I wasn't playing well.

So why am I writing you this letter anyway? Just to complain? Not really. Like I said, my golfing experience wasn't that bad. But it could have been so much better, and I see that so clearly now. I want to tell you, so you can learn from it. I don't want you getting to my age and feeling the same regrets I'm feeling now.

I wish, I wish. Sad words, I suppose, but necessary. I wish I could have played the game with more joy, more freedom. I was always so concerned with doing it right that I never was able to enjoy just doing it at all. I was so hard on myself, never satisfied, always expecting more. Who was I trying to please? Certainly not myself, because I never did. If there were people whose opinions were important enough to justify all that self-criticism, I never met them.

I wish I could have been a better playing partner. I wasn't a bad person to be with, really, but I wish I had been friendlier and gotten to know people better. I wish I could have laughed and joked more and given people more encouragement. I would have gotten more from them, and I would have loved that. There were a few bad apples over the years, but most of the people I played with were friendly, polite, and sincere. They just wanted to make friends and have a good time. I wish I could have made more friends and had a better time.

I'm inside a lot now, and I miss the beauty of the outdoors. For years when I was golfing, I walked through some of the most beautiful places on earth, yet I don't feel I really saw them. Beautiful landscapes, trees, flowers, animals, the sky, and the ocean—how could I have missed so much? What was I thinking of that was so important: my grip, my back swing, my stance? Sure, I needed to think about those sometimes, but so often that I was oblivious to so much beauty? And all the green—the wonderful, deep, lush color of green! My eyes are starting to fail. I wish I had used them better so I would have more vivid memories now.

So, what is it that I'm trying to say? I played the type of game that I thought I should play, to please the type of people that I thought I should please. But it didn't work. My game was mine to play, but I gave it away. It's a wonderful game. Please, don't lose yours. Play a game that you want to play. Play a game that gives you joy and satisfaction and makes you a better person to your family and friends. Play with enthusiasm, play with freedom. Appreciate the beauty of nature and the people around you. Realize how lucky you are to be able to do it. All too soon your time will be up, and you won't be able to play anymore. Play a game that enriches your life.

Best wishes . . . don't waste a minute of golf . . . someday it will be gone!

Signed,
Me"

INTRODUCTION

"If you want to be different, you need to do different."

—OPRAH WINFREY

It's January first, but it does not matter what year it is. The story is the same. This is the year I am going to be a scratch golfer. December 31st, and again, it doesn't matter the year, I am still not a scratch golfer. I have about the same handicap as I did when I started out the year. Where did I go wrong? I know I just need something different, and everything will click. There is a magic bullet. I know it. I must believe. This sums up the last forty years of my quest. Maybe it is an unattainable journey. Maybe I didn't work hard enough. Maybe I am getting too old. I'm not sure, but regardless I am still not a scratch golfer. The closest I have been is a 1.8 index. This was only for a brief moment in time. I could not play to it and lost a lot of money when I had it.

That index was not an indication of my ability, I just shot two good tournament scores. The handicap system can be brutal, but that is a different story. That year, I was the contributor to all golf bets. It was an expensive year.

I have spent more than forty years, although I cannot really remember that far back, saying to myself, *What I need is more distance, more consistency, a better short game, better putting, a stronger mental game, better game management, better bunker play, better data, and so on, and so on.* Today I still need all of those things. In my mind, I never achieved any of my goals, even though I went from a twenty handicap to a 1.8. I am now up to a 7.4. This book is not a psychology book, although it is obvious that I need one. This book is about all the ways I have tried to achieve all of these things. Most of what I have attempted borders on the absurd . . . or the insane. I wonder if you have done many of the same things. My journey has gone on, year after year, different approaches after different approaches, change after change, and excuse after excuse. The more I changed, the more I stayed the same. Let's be clear: I am not bitter. I love that I have been able to play all these years. What I lacked in talent I made up for in experimentation. I am a member of the lost and found club. I go to the driving range, and I find the answer. The next day, I lose it. Searching to find it again. I wonder if trying all these things made the game more interesting to me. Hard to know.

A little history about me. I am not sure why I started to play golf. I do know why I became addicted to golf. I remember that when I was in junior high school, there was a par-three golf course adjacent to a pizza place that we all used to hang out at. Occasionally, we used to hit golf balls at that golf course's range. We then played the course every so often. I did not have the money to play golf, but I always thought it was fun. I also remember playing a few times in college. Again, I had a lot of fun. I was lucky because I was a fairly good tennis player and played a lot of table tennis, so I had good hand–eye coordination. The first time I played a true eighteen-hole course, I remember that I broke a hundred. To be clear, I doubt that I truly recorded every stroke. Regardless, I could move the ball around the course. I thought golf was incredibly fun, but I was playing college tennis, working, and going to school. I didn't have much time to play.

When I graduated from college, I went to work for a large accounting firm. Most of the guys in my group played golf, so I got more interested in playing. I became extremely interested in playing when a good friend of mine, who was a scratch golfer, was invited to play Cherry Hills (a prestigious golf club in Colorado) with several partners and a high-powered client. I was left sitting at the office, working. It was at that moment that I decided to become a scratch golfer so I would be invited to play. From playing competitive tennis, I knew the importance of practice, so I started hitting as many balls as I could afford. This is when I became addicted. On the range, I could hit all kinds of shots. When I hit what I thought was a good shot, I just loved how it felt and what the ball did. Repeatability is a different question. The challenge of being able to hit it consistently got me addicted. I love playing golf, and I always love hitting balls on the range.

In my first year, I was shooting consistently in the low nineties. I figured that getting to scratch would take a couple of years but was very achievable. *The ball just sat there and never moved. Getting to be a scratch golfer cannot be that hard.* I played tennis at a fairly high level, so I figured my athletic skills were going to be good enough. I never thought about taking lessons. Couldn't afford it if I had. Honestly, when I finally did take a lesson, the game became extremely complicated. Before lessons, it was simple: Hit the ball.

As I look back at my forty-year journey, I realize that I just repeated the same cycle over and over again. *Chasing, what I need is this . . .* Talk about a habit. The number of variations to this statement is never ending. The number of things I have tried to resolve this statement is also never ending. When I look back over those forty years, I laugh at what I have done and gone through. It really is absurd. Regardless of how absurd it was, it has been a lot of fun trying. I will keep on trying.

Okay back to a little more history. When I was with the accounting firm, we played on the weekends for six months a year. We didn't practice a lot, at least not compared to now. My friends loved golf, and we stayed up all night just to get in line to get a tee time at three in the morning. The person getting the tee time was the person who did not get lucky that night. Unfortunately, that was usually me. Playing weekend golf was standard for a long time.

After nine years, I took a job with one of my clients and moved to Greeley, Colorado. I now had enough money to join a golf club, the Greeley Country Club. I had dreamed of belonging to a club ever since I was a kid. As a kid, it was for tennis. Now it is for golf. It seemed that being able to easily play whenever I wanted to could be a big step in becoming a scratch golfer. I could play two days a week and practice anytime I wanted. My job kept me busy, and by then, I was married and had two kids. However, when golf season was open, I consistently played two to three times a week.

I then spent the next thirty years doing the same thing. Trying to improve and telling myself, *I only need this*... I would work on it for a little while and then change to another *I only need this*.

After thirty-five years, the big day finally came. I sold my company and decided to commit a significant amount of time to golf and chasing a goal since the day I started playing: becoming a scratch golfer. I had a dream that I would write a book that could help anyone become a scratch golfer. I was convinced, and still am, that golf instruction is flawed at its core. During this pursuit, I realized how little I understand about golf. I have also had a lot of ideas that would revolutionize golf, but quickly realized that I was just duplicating what is already being done. I have not yet figured out a process that could save us from playing the game as it was designed to be played: even par or better. My belief system told me that before I could write such a book, I needed to achieve that goal. Otherwise, I am just talking to the wind. Although I have not achieved that goal yet, I have a lot of time on my hands and always wanted to write a book, so I decided to write a book that discusses the multiple things I have tried to do to become a scratch golfer. When I look at everything I have done, I really must wonder what I could have accomplished if I had focused on something meaningful. We will never know.

As I am writing this, I think I have found the secret. I have found the secret multiple times. I played golf with someone the other day who I have not played with for more than five years. He reminded me that I told him I found the secret back then. *Hmmm, I am on my 7,439th swing change, the secret must be in one of these.* Hope is a wonderful thing. It keeps us going. Okay, let us be clear: Who knows what swing change I am on? The number grows every day. I am always trying something new. Sometimes it is a substantial change, but most times it is just a little tweak here or there. Today, what I need is more distance. Tomorrow, more consistency. The next day, a better short game. I can always putt better. My mind and game management need work. The list goes on. These are just the main headings. There are subcategories under each of these and, I am sure, subcategories under these.

I also need to make one point. I am trying to recall things for the past forty years, so my stories may not be 100 percent true—or even 50 percent true—but they are what I remember. So do not bother fact-checking me.

Is my story unique? I do not think so. I believe most people who regularly play golf would like to be a scratch golfer. This book is for those people who are chasing that dream or who have achieved that dream. Sadly, most people give up the illusion. I think most golfers have decided that it is better to have a higher handicap so they can win bets with their friends. That is not a great goal for improvement. When I watch people play, it does not seem like most of them are having fun. Yet, people keep coming back. Not everybody, but enough to keep the game alive.

This book will not make you a better golfer. My hope is that you will laugh at what I have gone through. You might see yourself in some of these stories or just laugh at the absurdity of what I have gone through and be thankful you were not so foolish. Regardless, if I bring a smile to your face, and even an occasional laugh, I will have accomplished my goal.

After forty years, I still believe I could be a scratch golfer. Maybe not from the tips. The answer is simple. *I just need* . . . I have said that for more than forty years. But swing change number 7440 is different. Just as this year is different, and I will become a scratch golfer. It is possible. Nothing like a little positive affirmation and hope. Enjoy the journey.

MY QUEST

"Golf is the closest game to the game we call life. You get bad breaks from good shots; you get good breaks from bad shots—but you have to play the ball where it lies."

—BOBBY JONES

I want to be a scratch golfer. I think most of us who are serious about the game do. The problem is we are just not that good. (Less than 1 percent of all golfers play to a zero handicap or less). I have spent more than forty years on this quest. Hopefully, it is not over. I wonder why it was so important to me. Probably a little too late for that now.

Before I tell you about my endless journey of doing the same thing over and over again and expecting a different outcome, I thought you might want to know why I want to be a scratch golfer. Okay, I will be honest: I have no idea why it is so important to me. Maybe it is just ego. It is a goal I cannot let go. I have become a crazy addict. I really do not know why, but I do. I love the game, and I want to play the game the way it is supposed to be played. I have done it four times in my life, and it was an amazing experience each time.

A scratch golfer is playing the game the right way. It says that the golf course is not beating you. You are not beating the golf course, either. Of course, sometimes you do and sometimes you don't, but over time, you are evenly matched. The enjoyment of shooting under par is amazingly satisfying. I have done it twice. It would have been three times, but I hit the wrong ball, and that is another story. I have also shot even par twice. I know I am being selfish, but I want to play without worrying about a swing change or if I can hit a shot. I want to play, hitting shots and watching the shots do what they are supposed to do. I want my mind to play the golf course and not focus on my physical abilities. Finally, when asked, *How many strokes do you get?* I want to confidently say, *Zero*, and have everyone look at me in awe. All of you serious golfers know that if I became a scratch golfer, I would want to be a plus one or better, but that is irrelevant to this discussion.

When I started this quest, I did not realize how hard it is to become a scratch golfer. It is very hard. Here are some facts to put things into prospective. I know we should not let facts get in the way of a dream, but remember I am an ex-accountant. According to the United States Golf Association (USGA), 1.60 percent of the two million United States men who have established a handicap carry a handicap of zero or better. That means there are only thirty-two thousand male golfers in the United States who can play a golf course as it is designed. The statistic for women is even worse. These numbers do not even start to indicate how pathetic humans are as golfers. Only 7.5 percent of golfers have an official handicap. I am assuming that if you do not have a handicap, you are not a scratch golfer. Doing a little math, there are only thirty-two thousand golfers out of 26.6 million people playing golf who can consistently shoot around par or better. It appears that either we just are not very talented or golf is really hard.

I keep talking about being a scratch golfer. Those of you who just picked up the book for a little entertainment might not know what it means to be a scratch golfer. Basically, it means that you played eighteen holes of golf by taking exactly the number of strokes the course designer intended it to be played in. A par score is designated for every hole based on the length of the hole, and it assumes that two putts will be needed on every green. Therefore, a par four means that you should be able to hit the green in two shots, and it takes two putts for the ball to go in the hole. A par five means that it should take three shots to hit the green and two putts. Most eighteen-hole golf courses are either a par seventy-two or a par seventy. The difference is how many par five holes the course has.

However, there are always variations. So, being a scratch golfer means you played the course as it the designer intended it to be played. You can also play the hole better than it was designed. You can make one putt instead of two. You can hit a par five in two shots instead of three. You can hole out a shot on a par three or a par four. There are also a lot of ways to shoot a higher score than what was intended. The ways to do this are too numerous to describe. I have experienced these variations over and over and over again.

So, why do I think I could be a scratch golfer?

This is where either my ego or my incredibly optimistic attitude comes into play. I am a reasonably good athlete and have good hand–eye coordination. There is nothing that says I cannot be a scratch golfer. I even have some data to prove my point.

- I play the same golf courses all the time. I should know exactly where to hit the ball, how the greens break, and so on. I have no excuses for not understanding the golf course.

- I have birdied every hole on the courses I play. Numerous times!

- I do not play the tips; I usually play one up. Okay, now it is two up. So, distance is not really a problem. One of the beauties of golf is that you can cheat and make the course easier. It hasn't helped.

- When calculating a handicap, only the eight best scores out of the last twenty are counted. Think about it: You only count 40 percent of your attempts. Could they make it any easier? They justify this by saying your handicap is your potential. Who are they kidding? They just want you to feel better about yourself. It works; however, there is money involved. Only a fool bets on potential. *Hmmmm.*

- You do not have to count all your strokes. The maximum number of strokes you can take on any given hole is a net double bogey.

- Technology keeps improving. Changes in golf clubs and golf balls are allowing us to hit the ball farther by at least twenty to thirty yards and up to seventy yards for the driver (at least that is what I have heard.) I am struggling to hit my driver seventy yards these days. If you do not believe about all of the distance I should have gotten, just read the advertisements in a golf magazine. Better yet, find some clubs and balls that were made twenty years ago. Big changes.

- Golf course conditions continue to improve. It is difficult to find a bad lie in a fairway, and the greens are almost perfect. Everyone has gone to shaving the rough around the green, allowing people to putt the ball instead of chipping out of long rough. They say this is tougher, but I am not convinced.

- Clubs are perfectly fitted to our swing, and we no longer need to hit one, two, three, or even four irons. Hybrids have gotten rid of hitting these difficult clubs. This is especially beneficial to those with higher handicaps.

- The club head for my driver is three times bigger than it was twenty years ago, and drivers are made to reduce the spin to the point it is difficult to hook or fade a ball.

- I can dissect my swing at a level of detail never experienced before. I can take video of my swing and compare it with the greatest golfers in the world. My instructor can see what I am doing wrong and can visually show me.

- I can get a new tip and trick to improve my game every day. I can get thousands of them. *Hmmm, that might be problem number 1.*

- Golf training aids that can help me find the perfect swing have grown at an exponential rate. They say that all of these aids have been scientifically tested to improve my game. Of course, I believe them. They would not lie, would they?

- We know the importance of physical fitness. Get into better shape, and your golf game will surely get better.

Seeing all of this, it is impossible to understand why I am not a scratch golfer. Considering all of the changes and how few scratch golfers there are, it is hard to believe that anyone at all was a scratch golfer twenty years ago.

What is interesting is that with all of the improvement in technology and teaching methods, professional golfers have not gotten that much better either. The Vardon winners, the PGA professional with the lowest stroke average, had a low of 67.79 by Tiger Woods and a high of 69.61 by Matt Kuchar. The average for the last twenty-five years is 68.79, and the median is 68.96. Is it because they continue to make golf courses harder and harder for the pros, or is there another reason? Personally, I think putting a ball into a four-and-a-quarter-inch cup may be the biggest reason. It is just not that easy to make a putt. However, I am still surprised that this number has not dropped a lot more since the top players are playing par-sixty-eight golf courses. They can hit most of the par fives in two, and sometimes one or two par fours in one. But what do I know?

So why am I not a scratch golfer? I wish I knew the answer. When you read my journey, you will see that I have no clue. However, I have decided to defy Albert Einstein and keep trying the same thing over and over again, then wake up and say, "Hey that worked!" When I do, I will die before I get a chance to tell anyone.

You will see a consistent pattern when I explain my journey. Buy new clubs, get a training aid, take a lesson, etc. When I get into the mental game, it gets deep. Hard-core stuff. Okay, onward to my journey.

WHY DO I MAKE GOLF HARD?

"Golf is a hard game to figure. One day you will go out and slice it and shank it, hit into all the traps and miss every green. The next day you go out and, for no reason at all, you really stink."

—BOB HOPE

I have spent my life walking, throwing, and catching a ball. I have hit balls with different instruments like a bat and a tennis racquet. I have thrown balls into hoops and darts at a target. This just names a few activities. I have also done physical activities, like chopping down a tree, chopping firewood, pounding nails with a hammer, and sawing wood. I can do these things at varying levels of proficiency. In all cases, it took me some time and repetition to catch on to what I needed to do. We are talking minutes or, at the most, a couple of hours before I could perform the skill at some level of proficiency. Catching a ball took a little more time, however I was young when I learned how to do this. Hitting a ball with a bat or a tennis racquet in the direction I wanted it to go took a little more time. It did not take me a lifetime. In all cases, I stopped thinking about the mechanics and focused on the objective at hand.

If I am hammering a nail, my focus is on hitting the nail with a hammer in the right direction so it will go into the wood. I am amazingly successful at getting this done, considering I am swinging a heavy object with a small head and hitting a small object straight down so it goes in straight. Now, I am not as good as someone who has been pounding nails for the past thirty-five years, but I can hold my own. If I hammered a nail the way I try to play golf, I would never get the nail into the wood. When you hit a nail, do you think about how far you should take the hammer back, how much should you bend your wrist, and when are you going to release your wrist? No, you grab the hammer and you hit the nail. The first couple of times you may not hit it right, but very quickly, you are hitting the nail very consistently and you are hitting it harder and harder.

I remember when I first started playing golf, I picked up a club and started to hit a golf ball. No one showed me the right grip and all of the theoretically correct positions in the golf swing. I hit balls on the driving range. My objective was to hit the ball as far as I could in the right direction. After a couple of sessions, I could tell that I was doing something wrong and asked someone for help. Luckily, the only thing they told me was how to hold a club so I could hit the ball with some power. After that, I just practiced and played. Within two years, I was shooting in the low to mid-eighties. It took me another three years to get into the seventies. For two of these years, I shot eighties and eighty-ones fairly consistently. I only needed to bogey the last hole or last two holes to get into the seventies. Then, *bang!* my head would explode, and I would have a double bogey or triple bogey. I then went into the bar and told everyone my sad story. My very sad story. No one seemed to cry. Insensitive people. Golf was telling me that it is a mental game. I wasn't listening.

I finally broke into the seventies when I shot a seventy-six. I was so far under eighty that even I could not screw it up. After that, I started shooting in the seventies about half the time I played. However, I quickly plateaued and wasn't getting any better. I am not sure what my handicap was. I am guessing around an eight or nine. Remember, I was supposed to be a scratch golfer by then, and I wasn't even close. I decided to up the game and started to take lessons, started reading a lot of golf books, and started to change my swing. I had to change my swing to get better, didn't I? I entered the world of mechanical golf and swing prison (this term was from Steve Yellen in *Simplicity*, and I think it is the perfect description) at the same time. This decision changed my life, but not my golf game.

It all started with my first book (remember, the Internet didn't exist back then, so you could only read books or take personal lessons): *The Five Fundamentals of Golf* by Ben Hogan. My scratch golfer friend recommended this book. *The Five Fundamentals* was considered the bible back then, and it still is. I read it and tried to follow it. However, I don't think I really understood the basic concepts. It then occurred to me that since Jack Nicklaus is the best golfer ever, maybe I should read his book. This is where trouble first began. Ben Hogan and Jack Nicklaus have different concepts. They had different swings. I didn't understand this then, and I was trying to do two completely different types of swings at the same time. Not good.

The saga continued when someone suggested that I take a lesson from the pro at the Denver Country Club. First, the Denver Country Club is a very exclusive club in Denver. I was a public-golf course player. At that time, I had never played at a private country club. Very intimidating. Furthermore, I had never had a golf lesson before. I had no idea what was going to happen. So, I showed up, and just like every instructor, he asked me what I was trying to do. I do not remember exactly what I said, but I was thinking, *I want to shoot lower scores.* He said hit a couple of balls and let us see what is going on. I hit some balls that I thought were well hit. He looked at me and said, "Are you willing to start at the beginning? There is nothing good about your swing."

What? I was shooting consistently in the low eighties, which is in the top 20 percent of the golfing world. I was extremely disappointed, and I decided to drink the Kool-Aid. I said, "I want to do it right, so show me." I took three lessons from him and got worse. For the first time, I was thinking about all of these positions, what my body was doing, what my feet were doing. I have never recovered. The sad thing is, most of what he was teaching me was different from both Hogan's and Nicklaus's books. *What the hell is going on?*

I did not give up, and I still haven't given up. I have taken lessons from various pros, read multiple books, and got hooked into the online video world (there are thousands of different videos). They are all teaching something different. I try them all. Thousands of dollars and hours later, I haven't gotten dramatically better.

It is now thirty years later, and I am not that much better than I was after my first five years. Do I hit the ball better? Yes! Do I putt better? Yes! Is my short game better? Yes! Do I score better? Not really! Actually, right now I can hardly shoot in the seventies. I am not buying the old-age thing.

I wonder why I stopped making significant improvements in my game. The answer is obvious: I started down the track of *I need more . . .* I started trying to learn how to play golf the right way. I have seen this happen with other people as well. They start taking lessons, and they go backward. Instructors justify this with the statement that you need to get worse before you get better. That sounds like a bad teacher making an excuse. Yet, most of us buy into it. I wonder which makes less sense, the instructor saying it or me believing it?

Once you enter swing prison, the world becomes "if, only if." This thought process is an addiction. Golf needs something similar to Alcoholics Anonymous. The addiction needs to be broken. Once addicted, few people can escape without quitting the game.

I am going to take you through my swing prison. If you are new to the game, please don't follow this path. I don't want you to go to swing prison. If you are already in swing prison and looking for a way out, you need to find another book.

ALL I NEED IS MORE DISTANCE

"Every shot counts, a three-inch putt counts the same as a 300-hundred-yard drive."

—HENRY COTTON

Golf pros say that when they ask a new student what they want to improve, most times the student says consistency. The pro knows they are lying; what they really want is to hit the ball an exceptionally long way.

We all know distance is the answer. If I could just hit it more than three hundred yards, I could really go low. Even if I cannot hit it that far, just another twenty or forty yards would help. I know that distance is my problem. Everyone hits it farther than me. I just do not know why I cannot hit it farther. There are so many answers to this question, and I believe them all.

I am sitting, watching the Golf Channel, and I see an ad for a new driver. Hit the ball farther by twenty or more yards. I start feeling a little anxious. I know if I can get those twenty yards, I can achieve my dream. I would do anything to achieve my dream. I finally break down and go to the golf store and try out the driver. I bring my old driver because I want to make sure I am getting the twenty additional yards. They are not going to fool me. Today, when you try out a new driver or any club, they can tell you how far you hit the ball. Before technology, you just went on feel. I wonder how many more drivers they sell now. Regardless, I was getting ten to fifteen yards more with this driver. Not twenty, but something. Hey, I am not going to be greedy. I have to buy it, and I do. Something changed, and all the distance disappeared. What happened? I wish I knew.

I cannot tell you how many times I have heard the following: "I can guarantee that if you adopt this move, you will increase your distance by twenty to forty yards"; "This driver will increase your distance by at least twenty yards"; or "Fix this one thing in your swing and your distance will increase another twenty yards." I wonder, why is it always twenty yards or some increment of twenty yards? Must be the science involved. Who knows, but I believe them all! I should be hitting the ball at least 425 yards. No, that's not true, it should be a thousand yards. Unfortunately, I am not hitting the ball any farther. Maybe I'm even hitting the ball shorter distances. *I must not be following the instructions properly.*

I love distance. I love the thought of distance. *Hmmm, I do not think I have ever really experienced true distance.* However, it is fun when you hit a great tee shot. It is also fun to hit a good iron shot that just explodes off your club. When you hit shots like this, you feel like there is a chance to become a good golfer. Then you play with someone who really does hit it long. You say to yourself, *I need to find a way to hit it longer.* It does not matter that I beat them by five shots, my game needs more distance.

Is distance important? Yes! The closer you can hit the ball to the hole, the shorter your next shot is. The shorter the shot is, the easier it is to knock it close to the hole. The closer you are to the hole, the better your chance of making the putt. The more putts you make, the better your score. If your long game is good enough that you can reach the par fives in two, you have effectively reduced par for the course. Bryson DeChambeau can reach almost all par fives in two. He is playing par-sixty-eight courses. If you cannot reach the par fives in two, you are spotting him four shots. Hitting the ball a long distance is a big advantage, but you still must hit it relatively straight. If you hit it long but you are constantly in trouble or hitting it out of bounds, you give up all your advantage. With that said, a hundred-yard shot out of the rough is a much easier shot than a two-hundred-yard shot from the middle of the fairway. Why do you think the PGA pros bomb it as far as possible?

So, I want more distance. How do I get it? I have taken four paths in my endless journey. There are multiple segments to each of these paths. Remember, my journey is an endless cycle, so I do the same things year after year after year after year. I wonder if I am missing something. The four paths are:

- Get new clubs: This is always the simplest answer.

- Buy some training aids: You can't really make a change without a training aid.

- Fix swing flaws: Hard to believe that I have a swing flaw. It is possible.

- Get into better shape: The last resort.

Get new clubs

This always is the easiest answer. Just pay the money, and magically, you get another twenty yards. Amazing stuff.

Club manufacturers would not lie, would they? Every year they come out with a new driver that guarantees to give you an additional twenty yards. TaylorMade had all of their players wear a hat that said "20," meaning they were getting an additional twenty yards using their R9 driver, or was that the R11, 13, 14, or 15? Maybe it was not their R series but their Burner models or their Rocket Ballz model. Now that was a great name. If you hit a great drive, everyone said, "Rocket ballz." Now it is the Sim model. Callaway has the Epic, the Flash, and now the Epic Flash. I cannot remember them all. I have owned at least fifteen to twenty different drivers. I am still looking for that twenty yards. I think they should be banned from Google for misinformation. Unfortunately, once you are addicted, you believe whatever they tell you. Addiction is not a good thing. I just finished trying a new driver used by the long-drive guys. Maybe this is the answer. *What am I doing?*

It does not end with drivers; all of the brands kept coming out with new and improved sets of irons when people were hitting these clubs one club longer. They just forgot to mention that they are calling a club with a 31 percent loft a seven-iron when it was called a six-iron. What is absurd is we keep calling irons nine, eight, seven, and so on, instead of what degree of loft it is. The manufacturers do not want to talk about degree of loft. That would give away their secret. You would think we would demand that they change, but in truth, we like the idea of hitting seven-irons farther. If we hit the same loft, we would never hit it farther. Ignorance is bliss.

The truth is the USGA has defined the specifications for driver-club head. So, every driver being made for the last twenty years has been made at the maximum specification allowed. If the driver is at its maximum specification, where does all of this additional distance come from? *Hmmm, there is not any extra carry distance. Maybe some roll distance, because they are taking all the spin out.* It is all a big lie. Yet, I keep believing. I keep buying. Deep down, I know I need a new driver.

Okay, the driver specifications are maxed out, but the other clubs aren't. *Makes sense, doesn't it?* It amazes me that, in its wisdom, the USGA does not define specifications for any other club, only the driver. The PGA pros are now hitting their three woods more than three hundred yards and seven-irons more than two hundred yards. Regardless, I should definitely buy the clubs that are being juiced up. *Hmmm, why am I not getting the same benefit? Maybe it's the swing?* That cannot be possible.

Nope, it is not the swing. I need to get my clubs custom-fitted. When I first started playing golf, it seemed like most people just went to the store and bought a set. At least that is what I did. That really is not acceptable. You need the correct shaft, the right lie angle for your swing, and the right spin rate. Today, I would not consider buying a club without it being custom-fitted. There is so much technology available to determine if you are getting the right spin rate, the right smash factor, or whatever else they deem is important that you just cannot risk not getting your clubs custom-fitted.

Although I make fun of what I have done, I will say that getting your clubs fitted for you is one of the best things you can do. You do not want to wear shoes that do not fit. This is the same concept. There is a 100-percent certainty that whatever you buy off the shelf is not a good fit.

Luckily, my addiction for new golf clubs did not start until later in my golfing career. That was because I could not afford them before. However, today I am addicted to new clubs, and my mind is screaming at me to stop. I decided the answer was to buy really expensive clubs, so that way, I would not be tempted to buy a new set every year. I have a friend who buys one or two sets every year. When I bought the expensive clubs, he told me I was crazy. I told him if I only buy a new set every three years, I am ahead of him. So far, I am holding to this three-year cycle, but I am starting to break. Wish me luck.

Every time I get a new set of clubs, and I know I am going to hit the ball longer. I am so excited to hit these new clubs, especially the driver. I run out to the driving range and hit with them. They are amazing, I cannot wait to take them to the course. I hit the ball longer and straighter. They are a real game-changer. I go out and play. *I am going low. Wait, I am hitting the ball just the same. I am not going low. Nothing has changed. The distance is the same.* Then the famous excuse comes out: "I need to get used to them." I ask myself, *Get used to what?* I have been lied to, once again. *Okay, three thousand dollars gone, what is next?*

Hey, I just watched an ad for a new training aid.

Buy some training aids

There are hundreds of gadgets and gizmos to help you increase the speed of your golf swing. I think I have owned them all. There is a fan, speed sticks, heavy clubs, light clubs, arm weights, and the list go on. Do training aids really work? It's hard to tell, they have never really changed my game. However, I keep buying new ones, so they must.

My first training aid for speed was a fan. I just want you to know that there are a lot of training aids for distinct parts of the game. I am just going to talk about the ones that are for hitting it longer for now. You will have to wait patiently for the others.

1. The fan is a club that has four wings on it. It creates air resistance. The idea is that if you swing the fan hard, it creates resistance, which builds up your strength in the areas that create speed. It is a good workout. However, if you have a bad swing, you are training the wrong muscles anyway. Also, you might just hurt yourself by swinging so hard. People always teach you to let it go and not fight it. This is the exact opposite. Which is right?

2. Next was the power club. This was a heavy-weighted driver. The basic theory is that you gain club-head speed by swinging something heavier than normal. It's the same theory as the fan. There is a different school of thought. This school says that you should swing something much lighter. *Come on guys, what is the real answer?* No one seems to know. It is a mystery. A good friend of mine loves the power club. He is one of the top ten senior golfers in Colorado. He would swing the power club as a warm-up on the first tee. It seems that 60 percent of the time, he would pull his first tee shot to the left. I told him that I thought swinging the

power club was causing the problem. He argued vehemently with me. He no longer uses the power club, and he does not hit it left anymore. *Hmmm.*

3. Increasing the length of my backswing. I bought a training aid that you would grip with your left hand and then grab a component with your right hand that moved toward the end of the club, giving you more extension. It was a good stretching aid, which I am guessing cannot hurt. But more distance? No.

4. Next came the speed sticks. These sticks have three different weights, heavy, regular, and light. You swing each weight ten times with a regular swing, a step-in swing, and a running swing (see the movie *Happy Gilmore*). It is a good workout, and the theory is teaching yourself to swing hard. There is a lot of science that says that once your body gets comfortable with a certain swing speed, you need to do something to break that comfort zone. It makes too much sense not to try it. I do have a friend that said he gained ten miles per hour of swing speed by going through the program. I must admit he is hitting it far. However, he always hit it far.

5. There is a gadget called the Orange Whip, and there are some variations. There is the Swoosh and the Lag Shot, just to name a couple more. The Orange Whip and the Swoosh have balls attached at the end of the shaft. With the Swoosh, the ball actually moves. The Lag Shot has a club head on it so you can hit a shot. These training aids are based on the concept of being better at sequencing, because the shaft is trailing significantly further behind you, since it is very flexible. I admit it does slow you down in the downswing. However, the feel of swinging this club is different from the feel of swinging your regular shafted club. Your subconscious mind knows the difference and modifies accordingly. So, does it really help? Who knows?

I could go on, but this covers the main concepts. Most people, and you can include me in this list, buy the training aid and use it a couple of times, then decide it did not really help. Obviously I just bought the wrong one.

I do believe that trainings aids are helpful—the reason I have a garage full of them—but they are so different that it is hard to tell which is right. The training aids for distance fit into three categories.

- An extra-light type of club

- An extra-heavy or high-resistance type club

- Something to help increase mobility

So, what gives you more swing speed? I know, a better swing. You would think that there might be some true science to tell you. Each product does give you their science explaining why it works, but how am I supposed to know? I buy all of the aids, and none of them seem to work like I think they should. I do not think any of them make the promise that if you do it once, you will be fixed. However, if it does not work the first time, you question the effectiveness of the tool. How can you keep using it then? I am guessing that using it once or even two or three times is not enough. That's unfortunate.

Okay, let's be honest: for some reason, I feel strange when I bring out a training aid. Everyone is looking at you, wondering, *What is that?* They are telling themselves, *He must need a lot of help on his game.* What they are really saying is, *I wish I had the guts to bring out that stupid contraption. I need more distance as well.* Then they go play with you and say, "You are not hitting any longer." They ask, "Is that training aid helping?" You say, "Oh yeah, but it takes time." The great excuse. I love that excuse.

There is no doubt that to get your subconscious to do something different you have to rewire your brain. Of all the training aids, I could not say that any of them truly helped my distance. I do think it if I really worked at the speed sticks that would help, because I would be trying to increase my body's internal code. I should also use the speed detector I bought so I actually know. However, if I do that I can no longer live in denial. Something to ponder.

I heard of a training aid I didn't think about. Buy new shoes. I was watching a commercial on the golf channel, and they said their shoes would increase my distance. Now this was a solution I was not even thinking of. Obviously, having the right shoe will give you more distance. There are currently two shoes that I know of that claim more distance with their shoes. *Who cares about comfort if I can hit it farther?* Now, they are only claiming five more yards. However, for five yards, I will do anything. I bought one of the brands, and I like them. About two months later, I was having a major pain in my hips. This continued for at least five months, and I was in a lot of pain. I did MRIs, acupuncture, massage therapy, chiropractic, and anything that I thought would help. I even bought a new bed. The new bed was the best thing I did. I finally found a physical therapist who asked me about my shoes. I realized the pain started about the same time I bought those shoes. The shoes are gone, the pain is almost gone, and I never did get my extra five yards.

Fix swing flaws

We watch the PGA pros hit their drives well over three hundred yards at sea level. The announcers say, "He has a two-hundred-yard shot and has a seven-iron." At one of my golf clubs, there is a guy who does not weigh more than 140 pounds and is only five feet six inches tall, and he hits his driver well over three hundred yards. Heck, some women on the LPGA tour that do not weigh more than 110 pounds are hitting it farther than me. A lot farther. If you watch their swings and see how big they are, you ask yourself, *How do they hit it so far?*

First, when I look at their swing and my swing, there are some definite differences. Now, I do not have a bad swing. Actually, a lot of people have told me that I have a good swing. *Why am I listening to a twenty handicapper?* I was convinced I had a good swing until I recently took a lesson from Mike Malaska. Mike is one of the top golf instructors in the world. He was named 2011 PGA National Teacher of the Year. Only the best for me. He told me that beside my grip, my posture, my takeaway, and my downswing, I have a good swing. (I am not really sure he said this, but that was the essence of what I learned.) He also said that if I did not have such good hand–eye coordination, I would not be able to hit a ball. When he said that, I truly laughed. Although I liked living in denial, hearing the truth can be freeing. Kind of like the Judge Simon Cowell on *America's Got Talent* and originally *American Idol*. He made me look at my swing on video, and there is something that is not right. I was not doing anything that I thought I was doing. He was right. Back to another swing change.

I thought Mike Malaska was going to get me to the promised land, and he might have; however, I found a new swing coach, Sam Randolph who is teaching at my club. I like what he is saying. My new guru. This will be my fifth or sixth teacher. Maybe this time is the charm. I do think that finding a good teacher to fix your flaws is a good idea. However, asking your friends what is wrong with your swing is definitely a better way to go. It's cheaper in the short run, but maybe not so cheap in the long run. To be honest, I am not sure exactly what a good golf instructor is. I guess it is someone you truly believe in. Twenty years ago, there were not a lot of options. Today there are numerous options. The Internet has saved golf. You can now sign up for online instruction and watch an endless number of tips and tricks, all promising you more yards. They break down the swing into every aspect, then you can video your swing, and they will analyze it and give you feedback. Which is the best way to go? I have come to learn that neither really works. *Maybe I should go back to asking my friends.*

I have always had an issue with golf instruction. The concept makes perfect sense, but the execution leaves a lot to be desired. I am going to share my thoughts. I have no good solution. I am just complaining to complain.

First, I assume that most PGA professionals loved golf and were good at golf but not good enough to make any money playing. They needed a job, so they say, *What the heck, let's become a professional.* The key word is they loved golf, which is a big difference from "I love teaching." I think very few professionals spend any time learning how to teach. The theory is, *If I am good, I should be able to teach.* There is nothing that says that statement is true. However, if you really do not like teaching, the chances are you are not very good. I have experienced some of these instructors. Here is my best example.

"Hello, what do you want to accomplish?"

"I want more distance."

"Okay hit a few balls. Hmmm, I have a trackman so we can measure what is going on."

I am thinking, *This is going to be good. Someone who is using technology.* Then I found out that he was borrowing it from a member and just testing it out. *Interesting.* I hit a few more balls, and he gives me my numbers.

He then says, "You have too much spin on the ball, and your angle of attack is not right. You need to hit more up on the ball."

I say, "Okay. How do I do that?"

He says, "Just move the ball up further in your stance."

I do, and my angle changes slightly, but my distance does not improve.

Then he says, "Let's just keep trying to hit more up on the ball."

I say, "Is there anything specific I should be trying?"

He says, "I'm not sure, but let's just keep working on it."

Nothing is changing. He then says, "Swing harder."

I thought everything was about an effortless swing? Okay, let's swing harder. I then get way out of balance. Obviously, I have something wrong going on. However, he has no advice. Needless to say, I never took another lesson from him.

Now that was a bad lesson. Most lessons are a little better and go like this.

"Hello. What do you want to accomplish?"

"I want more distance."

"Great. Let's hit a few balls," the pro says. "Hmmmm, okay let's try this . . . and see if that helps."

"That looked good. Now let's add this," he suggests.

Then, "You hit a bad shot. That happened because of this. Let's not do that anymore."

Finally he says, "Okay, you seem to be getting it. Now let's add this. Hit some more balls."

Then, "I think you should also try this."

Okay, I am now on four things I am thinking about. The lesson is over, and I diligently work on all four things. The problem is that no one is watching me, so while I think I am doing these things, I am not doing any of them. I now think of all these things when I am playing, and I start playing worse. And I go back to the pro, "What is wrong with my swing?" and the process starts again, and again, and again. I then decide that this is not working, so I change teachers. He or she has a different philosophy and is telling me completely different stuff. It does not work either. Now what?

Then comes the invention of digital swing instruction. I think that I just went to heaven. I was no longer limited to just books and magazine articles. I could spend my life watching everything. The first one I saw was Revolution Golf. A new swing tip every day! Just think, see a swing tip and go to the range to try it. And you screw up your swing just a little bit more.

There are a lot of different digital golf websites. Go to YouTube and search on golf swings. You could spend the next year just watching all of the different people. They are all different. They all have different thoughts and concepts. There is Rotary Golf, Clay Ballard, Tom Sarguto, Moe Norman, Steve Pratt, Mike Malaska, and the list goes on. All of these websites have amazing content of all the various positions they think you should be in. The coolest thing is they all promise me that I will get an extra twenty yards. All of them. Unfortunately, the same problem that exists with the PGA professional exists for these websites. Is the swing they are teaching right for you? What are the chances that you understand and can replicate what they are teaching? I have come to learn that those chances are very low. The one thing about digital instruction is these people do like to teach, and they try keep up to date with what the golf world is learning through technology. Your local teaching pro probably doesn't. However, the top digital instructors are also great marketers. *I wonder if they are lying to me.*

I know why I don't hit it long. Knowledge and execution are completely different.

Watch the pros play, they all have great balance, which allows them to accelerate the club through impact with the ball. Their swings are very efficient. Basically, they are able to maximize their speed because nothing in their swing is causing their subconscious to slam on the brakes. The same stuff that affects consistency also affects distance. The ability to hit the ball hard does not reduce your consistency. In a lot of ways, it improves consistency. Just watch the PGA pros. They are hitting it hard—extremely hard—and their accuracy is pretty amazing. When they miss, it seems like a huge miss, however, when compared to some of our misses, they are not really that big.

When you see my swing, I am slamming on the brakes. So how do you change your swing? It seems to be very difficult. To explain, here is a sad but funny story. I just went to the Moe Norman Golf School and was working hard on duplicating his swing. I thought I was pretty close. A friend of mine had a golf room where he could video my swing. I thought, *This will be great. I can see the new swing.* We videoed it, and I could not believe my eyes. It was my same old swing. *That is okay, I know what I am trying to do. I can change it right now. I am only going to change one thing.* I made the swing, and I know I did what I wanted to do. I watched the video. It was still the old swing. Nothing changed. *Okay let's try just taking it back halfway.* Nope still took it back too far. How do you change your swing when your conscious mind is thinking one thing, but your subconscious mind says, *Nope, we do not do it that way?* Don't tell that other mind. I wonder if the only way you can change is to have constant video or someone watching every swing. They (whoever they are) say you need to exaggerate or have a training aid to help you. A one-inch change can seem like ten feet. My mind is yelling at me to just give up, but I can't. I just need to try something else.

I believe that the number one rule in golf is you must swing in complete balance. Once you fall out of balance, even a little bit, your subconscious says, *Wait a minute, we might fall, so I am going to slam on the brakes. We do not like falling down.* Your subconscious really does not care if you hit the ball hard, but it does care that you do not hurt yourself.

The next rule of swing mechanics: Your backswing cannot exceed your ability to turn your shoulders. Once you take your backswing beyond your physical ability to turn, you will change the angle of your spine, and you will lose power and control. This is because you are repositioning your body, and you then break rule number one. Your body says, *We cannot go at it hard through the impact area because I need to get back into balance.* More power comes from being able to generate power through the impact area, not necessarily how far you take it back. Actually, there is no scientific evidence that taking the club back farther creates more club-head speed. A great example is Bruce Lee, who could break a board with his finger, moving it less than two or three inches. He was able to generate a tremendous amount of speed and power in a short distance.

You must create the most speed when you are hitting the ball. Most amateurs do not swing hard at the ball, they swing hard when they start their downswing. They create the most speed at the beginning of their downswing. By the time they get the club to the impact position, they are decelerating because they have no ability to sustain that speed. Great players have a smooth transition, and don't start generating their power until their hands have reached hip level. They are then able to generate a substantial amount of power in this small area, similar to Bruce Lee.

It is all so easy. Why can't I do it? I am stuck because I have developed a speed that my body is comfortable with. I must get unstuck. But how?

They say the best way to learn something is to do drills that help train your body to do something different. I have learned something about the body: It does whatever it wants to do. It does not like change. Therefore, most drills are an attempt to over-exaggerate what you are trying to do so your body will slowly start to make a change. However, when you do different drills and you truly over-exaggerate, it feels like there is no way you can ever hit a ball like this. I slowly get tired of hitting uncomfortable bad shots with the new swing and slowly revert to my more-comfortable bad shots with my old swing. The new swing didn't really fix anything. *How long do I need to do these drills anyway?* No one tells you. There must a simpler way.

Get into Better Shape

Okay, this must be the area of last resort. Get into better shape. What an absurd idea. Who has the time to do this? It sounds like a lot of hard work. Okay, let's think about this.

There are reasons professional golfers work out: It increases their strength and allows them to hit the ball farther. Not to mention Bruce Lee again, but it seemed like he was in tremendous shape. Most people would say that Tiger Woods started the physical-fitness craze in golf. While I believe that is true, when you look at any great golfer in the world, they are all good athletes. Jack Nicklaus was a good basketball player in addition to being a good golfer, and he had the opportunity to play for Ohio State University. Arnold Palmer was physically fit and strong. Look at Bryon Nelson and Ben Hogan; they were both in good shape. Now I know there are golfers like Craig Stadler, who obviously was not in great shape. However, I have seen some great college basketball players and some great football players on the offensive line who did not look like they were in great shape either. They were still great athletes.

Okay, I am buying in. I am going to get in better physical shape. What kind of physical shape? I decide that being in good physical shape for golf made the most sense. It is hard to understand how I figure this stuff out. I found someone who does this. He gave me a physical fitness test that determines your physical-fitness handicap. I was an eighteen. *Eighteen, are you kidding me?* They tried to make me feel better and said that this handicap does not relate to my golf handicap. I should get a participation trophy as well. They showed me that if I were not able to improve in certain areas of strength and flexibility, I would never be able to consistently hit certain golf shots. They said I could not maintain my balance during the swing. Remember, without great balance you will never hit it long or be consistent. Being told I was an eighteen physical-fitness handicap was like being told I have cancer and am going to die in the next year.

For more than forty years, I have had various levels of physical conditioning. I would say, from good to bad, but never great. I wonder, *At sixty-three years old, can I improve physically enough to become a scratch golfer?* Maybe. *Will I spend the effort to get into great shape?* Now that is hard work.

They say (again, whoever they are) that if you want to play better golf, improving flexibility, increasing core strength, and building better balance is critical. I had to ask why. Here are the answers they gave me.

1. You are trying to swing a club as quickly and as powerfully as you can, creating a lot of centrifugal force. The stronger you are, the more you can manage this force and stay in balance.

2. The stronger you are, the better you can handle difficult lies and difficult stances where you need strength to maintain your balance while you are swinging the club.

3. Good balance is related to having a strong core. Without good balance, it is difficult, if not impossible, to hit it long and straight.

They also said that the right kind of shape is important. For example, running may hurt your golf game because, when you run, you are building your muscles to move straight ahead, which can hurt your ability to move your hips laterally. A golf swing requires lateral movement, not straight ahead movement. It is all getting way too difficult.

If I were guaranteed that being in great physical shape would make me a scratch golfer, I might try to get there. However, it looks like Michael Jordon is in great shape, plus he is amazingly strong, and he is not a scratch golfer. I know he plays and practices a lot. See, that proves it, so I guess I won't bother getting into great shape. However, I am working on staying in good shape. I do not think great shape is in my future.

Okay, I hit it far enough. We always play one up from the back tees anyway. Okay, the combo tees. I know, what I need to work on is my consistency.

I NEED MORE CONSISTENCY!

"A golfer has to train his swing on the practice tee, then trust it on the course."

—BOB ROTELLA

The key to becoming a scratch golfer must be consistency. *I need to have a repeatable swing. I need to know where the ball is going every time I hit it. I just cannot afford to give away shots on the golf course. Brilliant.* I have only thought about this every year for the past forty years. Maybe I will listen this year. I just need to become more consistent. Okay, great, but how do I do that? Being a man of reasonable intelligence, I sit down and think about my options. This is what I came up with. *(I am thinking I might change golf forever.)*

- Get new clubs. I just need the right set of clubs.

- Find and fix my swing flaws. Obviously, there is something wrong in my swing that does not allow me to hit the ball the same way all the time.

- Go to the range and hit a lot of golf balls. Hitting more balls will improve my muscle memory and I will become significantly more consistent.

- Find a miracle training aid. Does one exist?

I have done all four, multiple times.

New clubs

Getting new clubs is the universal answer to all golfing problems. I know this is true. If I am playing someone who has clubs that are more than three years old, I know they are not very good. *How could they be? Who could be any good playing old clubs? How did Nicklaus and Woods manage with the clubs they were using? It's hard to even comprehend.*

Getting some new clubs is the easiest solution. Luckily, I can go to a demo day where I can try out all kinds of different clubs. I can hit these clubs on the range, compared to going to a store where I can only hit into a computer screen. I never truly believe the computer screen. Hitting into a digital net does give you all the cool stats, but it is just not the same. I know my clubs that are holding me back. *I got these clubs two years ago. Old technology. Who can play great golf with old technology? This is really going make a difference in my game.* I arrive and try out all kinds of clubs. Everyone tells me why their clubs are different and how I will be able to hit the ball farther and straighter with their clubs. I am trying different clubs, and I am hitting the ball as well as I have ever hit it. The ball is flying straight and long. It seems like I never miss a shot. Very exciting. I decide on a set of irons, a driver, and some fairway woods. The complete set. I do not want some old club to ruin my opportunity to become a scratch golfer.

I want the clubs I have been hitting with, but they will not let me have them. They are going to ship me the new set. The alarm clock goes off in my head. *How do I know that everything will be exactly the same?* The sale representative assures me that he has all the specifications, and I will be very happy. The problem is, I know that the shafts that are coming off the production line are going to be different than the ones I just hit. I have heard the deviation in clubs off the production line can be so extreme that a regular shaft, when measured, could be extra stiff or extra flexible. I am not happy, but what is a person to do? The clubs finally show up, and I know that my world is going to change. *I am winning the club championship this year.* I go out to play, and *What the hell? These clubs are not performing any better than the old clubs.* In some ways, they are even worse. *Something is wrong. I know these clubs are not the same as the ones I was hitting during demo days.*

I decide to take the clubs to a club-fitting company that will test the frequency or the relative stiffness of each club. The theory is that your shafts should have the same frequency that fits your swing. If you have different frequencies, you will modify your swing to compensate for the difference. Additionally, the distances for your irons will not be spaced out appropriately. Terrible things happen when you have different frequencies.

Sure enough, the shafts were not consistent, so I now must buy a whole new set of shafts. *This is starting to get expensive. However, becoming a scratch golfer is priceless, so let's go for it.* Again, the new clubs come, and I am extremely excited. The clubs do feel much better when I swing them. On the range, I am thinking to myself, *How did I ever hit a golf ball without these shafts?* Off to the course to play a round with these clubs. I limp into the nineteenth hole, shooting the same score I always shoot. Out comes excuse number one: I just need some time to get used to them.

I continued with these clubs until I sold my company. My employees gave me a gift certificate to have a set of clubs custom fit for me at TaylorMade. *Now we are getting somewhere.* I got fitted, and ended up buying a new driver, three-wood, and five-wood. He said my irons were just fine. *Really?!* It makes sense, since I did have the frequency of my irons checked. Again, everything was shipped to me, and again, I did not hit the ball any better. While I agree that your clubs should be fitted for your swing, obviously it is not the entire answer. So . . .

Swing flaws

I decide that I must have a swing flaw. I have read more than hundred different golf books. I just recently saw this saying that I loved: "The only thing you can learn from golf books is that you can't learn anything from golf books, but you have to read an awful lot of golf books to learn it."

I have tried at least thousand different tips and tricks from golf magazines and watched a Revolution Golf video at least once a day for more than two years. I am now hooked on YouTube videos about golf, each telling me they have the answer. I have taken lessons from six PGA professionals and twenty amateurs. I still wonder why I even consider listening to what a fifteen handicap is telling me. I am on swing change number 7,439. No, I have not really kept count. I am probably guessing low, but let's just go with it. After all of this, I cannot even tell what swing type I have. I am guessing I have some element of each. The pros I have taken lessons from say I have a good swing, except my new coach. At least he is truthful. My friends say I have a good swing. I am guessing they are just trying to be nice. When I watch someone who can play, their ball flight is just different than mine. *Hmmm, what does that mean?*

It is almost impossible to believe in what you are doing. Every so-called expert has a different thought. In my more than forty years (if you think that is a long time, it is), this is what I have learned: a lot of different swing ideas. The inconsistency in what is taught is amazing. What is more amazing is that a lot of what is being taught is hurting people, not helping them. I do not believe that anyone is purposely trying to provide bad information, but they have no science or, for that matter, common sense about what they are saying. The profession is all about fixing the symptoms. They do not seem interested in fixing the root cause, and then maybe tweaking from there. I believe that PGA professionals are teaching what they think is right. However, there was a time when scholars taught people that the world was flat and the best medical minds in the world bled people to cure them. Did you know that George Washington died from strep throat? The doctors bled half his blood to get rid of it. It worked: he died. Now we all know that the world is round and bleeding people to cure something is insane, but how long did it take numerous scholars, the nobility, and the rest of humanity to change their beliefs? I read that it took thirty-five years before people accepted the cure for the plague, and millions of people were dying. No one is dying from bad golf instruction, so why should it ever change? Good question.

Okay, enough of my rant. The plan is to find a good teacher. This does seem like the most logical thing to do. The first problem with that plan is there are more than twenty different basic types of swings. Here are some examples. I know there are more, but I have not found them.

- **The simple swing**: Turn back and through, and the arms naturally follow on the same plane. Also called the one-plane swing.
  - ▸ Great for short players
  - ▸ Requires good balance because of the speed it generates
  - ▸ Tends to be left-arm dominated

- **The tall-player swing**: Stand tall, stay on plane with the beginning shaft angle, and keep everything level through clearance. This is the one used by Greg Norman.
  - ▸ For a tall player, it seems like the ball is four inches below your feet
  - ▸ Balance, as always, is critical

- **The turn-and-lift swing**: Turn and then lift your arms, and then turn and lift your arms on the follow-through. This is the one used by Tom Watson.
  - ▸ Definite separation between body and arms
  - ▸ Shoulders turn horizontal on backswing and arms are lifted high
  - ▸ Hips turn through more quickly
  - ▸ The follow-through tends to be more vertical
  - ▸ Good for people who over hook the ball

- **The up-and-over flat swing**: Club starts to the left and then comes across the body. This is the one used by Lee Trevino.
  - ▸ The left hand is flat
  - ▸ You end up in a position where you can hit the ball with your right hand from an inside position
  - ▸ This type of flat swing normally creates a push, which is why Lee Trevino always aimed way left of the target
  - ▸ Similar to the lift-and-turn swing
  - ▸ Results in a very swallow swing

- **The hands-and-wrist swing**: Wrists are fully cocked, and the club will clearly rest on the left thumb. This is the one used by Fred Couples.
  - ▸ A fluid-looking swing
  - ▸ A full and complete turn of the hips
  - ▸ On the downswing, there is the feeling of releasing the wrists
  - ▸ Cupping of the left wrists
  - ▸ Very much a timing swing
  - ▸ If the body leads, you tend to hit a fade or a slice
  - ▸ If the legs lag, you tend to hook it
  - ▸ Feeling of waiting for it

- **The drawer swing**: At the end of the swing, the knees and the hips are still facing slightly right of the target.
  - ▸ The legs and hip stay well back through the backswing
  - ▸ Not a lot of leg movement through the ball.
  - ▸ Looks like the swing is restricted
  - ▸ Good for players with a stronger build, with minimal leg action
  - ▸ Everyone wants to hit a draw

- **The cutters swing**: A steeper swing with a definite out-to-in path.
  - ▸ A quick hip turn
  - ▸ Lose distance
  - ▸ Tends to be a safe shot
  - ▸ If you get too quick with your hands, you will have a pull hook
  - ▸ You can control a cut

- **High and wide**: Takes the club straight back and high with the famous right elbow. This is the one used by Jack Nicklaus, arguably the best player ever.
  - ▸ Low head position, steep shoulder turn, and high arm position
  - ▸ The right hand cannot release
  - ▸ Few can get to the inside with this swing, as Nicklaus is one of the few who did

- Tends to cause back problems

- **Togetherness**: Left elbow folds inward as compared to outward. This is the one used by Bernhard Langer, the best senior player ever.
  - Both backswing and follow-through stay on the exact same path
  - Rare swing, because most people cannot keep the left elbow in, and if there is any spread, then you will block it to the right

- **Right-sided swing**: A full-body turn with resistance against the legs. This is the one use by Nick Faldo.
  - Good for tall players
  - Hit with the right side of the body, but the arm and the wrist must be held back
  - Flatter back swing
  - Considered a complex swing

- **The majestic finish:** Low backswing, but follow-through is high. This is the one used by Seve Ballesteros.
  - A swing based on feel
  - Head finishes higher than when he started

There are also swing types for your body type, like the leverage swing, the arc swing, and the width swing. Bryson DeChambeau has created his own swing type, which is based on a one-plane swing made famous by Moe Norman. Moe's, however, was closer to a simple swing. Listing all these swings shows the craziness of golf. Who knows what the professional you are working with is teaching? I am not even sure they know what they are teaching. *Which swing is best for me? How do I know?* With all the books I have read and videos I have watched, my guess is I have created my own swing. It is called the seven-handicap swing. It is not really that good. I wonder if I could write a book about it. Well, I could, but who would buy it?

Hit lots of ball at the driving range

So, I know what to do and what not to do, and now I am going to ingrain these into my body and my mind. I need to spend time on the driving range. I mean a lot of time. The driving range is the place where swings are transformed, and consistency is built. You must hit ball after ball after ball if you are ever going to develop a great swing. Developing a great swing is not enough, though, you also must create muscle memory so you can repeat the swing consistently. Funny, there is no such thing as muscle memory. But why let science get in the way of a good theory? There is no documentation that

I can find of when the first driving range was created. My guess, it was a United States invention, since most courses in Scotland still do not have a driving range. Saint Andrews had to create a driving range that is about a mile away from the course. Players used to hit balls into a pasture and then go pick them up themselves. There is a terrific book called *Afternoons with Mr. Hogan: A Boy, A Golfing Legend and the Lessons of a Lifetime,* written by Jody Vasquez. Jody was a ball boy who used to shag Hogan's balls for him. Hogan used to practice on the actual golf course. How great would that be? Might slow down play, if you let everyone do that. I wonder if the driving range was just a great idea to make a lot of money and was not about improving your game at all.

I think driving ranges are great. I love hitting balls, because you get into such a rhythm that every shot is perfect. People are constantly saying that if they could just take their driving range swing onto the course, they would be a scratch golfer. I have always wondered where that swing goes. I believe my swing at the range looks the same as it looks on the course. It just seems like the results are different. Maybe it isn't the swing; maybe it is something else. I never really work on the something else, or even really tried to figure out what that something else is. Why would I, as that would be common sense?

I am 100 percent confident that if I cannot hit the ball well on the driving range, I have some major problems with my swing. Think about it: there is no pressure. Who really cares where the ball goes. On the range, I am hitting the same shot five to ten times or more with the same view and the same lie (perfect). This will be the best I am going to hit the ball. So, if it is bad on the range, it's going to be bad on the course. Rarely does something magical happen on the course. When playing, I only get one swing, I have different views, the lies are not perfect, and, if I miss it, it could result in an additional stroke—if not more than one. There really is not a comparison between hitting a golf ball on a driving range and on the golf course.

Driving ranges do allow you to work on your swing. You can build strength in your body. Making a hundred swings in thirty to sixty minutes is working your body and building strength and flexibility. It is no different than doing hundred push-ups. Strength and flexibility are important when playing a round of golf. Second, hitting a lot of good shots does help your confidence. It allows you to tell yourself, *I can hit this shot. I have hit it a hundred times on the driving range.* Third, driving ranges allow you to see the immediate effects of trying to make a swing change. The dichotomy is if you work on different swings every time you go to the driving range, you are not really accomplishing anything. You are just hitting balls. Note to self: For the past forty years, I have just been hitting balls. But hey, it is fun.

They say that you should try to hit different shots on the driving range. Hit low hooks, high fades, straight balls, and so on. This is helping you learn what you need to do in these situations. Try to play your course on the driving range. That's great advice, but I'm not sure I have ever seen anyone do this. Work on the same swing. Try to recognize the feeling of your swing. If you think you need to make a swing change, just make it and then stick with it. This is from the guy who is on swing change number 7,439.

Find a magical training aid

I cannot do this by myself. I need to find a training aid, a magical one. You might ask, "Are there training aids that help you build consistency?" I have tried a lot of training aids, and they all say they do. I haven't found one yet that really works.

Most consistency training aids seem to focus on getting you into the right position at the top. They are all focused on where your arms, hands, torso, and wrists should be. It is curious because all of the great teachers and players say the golf swing should be a continuous motion, not fixed positions. I am not sure that trying to get into a certain position is continuous. *I must be missing something.*

There are also some training aids where you can hit the ball. I always like these the best. I think there is a basic problem with training aids. They all seem to focus on your arms and hands, not what your feet and legs are doing. That is interesting to me because they say what your feet and legs are doing is the starting point for any good golf swing. The theory is that if you can get your feet, knees, and hips to work correctly, the upper body will do what it needs to do. Chuck Quinton with Rotary Golf created Axiom. He states that you just need to focus on your right foot moving in a clockwise circle. It does seem to work. However, for some reason, I always seem to forget this concept.

Here are some of the crazy training aids I have purchased:

- A ball that is attached to a strap that goes around your neck. You put the ball in between your elbows and hit the ball, taking half swings. Basically, you swing a club with a ball in between your elbows. The idea is to teach you to stay connected. Works great for half swings, but not so well for full swings.

- A vest that is supposed to keep everything together. It might have been okay, but it was hard to put the vest on. Again, it restricts your swing.

- There are all kinds of gadgets that, in theory, will put your hands in the right position at the top and through the downswing. Some examples are Precision Impact and Swingyde.

- There are clubs where the ball will not go right unless you hit the ball properly at impact. I like these because you feel like something positive is actually happening. The problem never seems to translate to the course, though. Very confusing.

- My most recent purchase is called a divot mat. This shows you exactly what your divot looks like when you swing the club. I like this mat, however I cannot seem to make the same divot twice. Do you think that is telling me something? Can this be affecting my consistency? Hmmm.

Hitting the ball consistently seems hard. You know, if I just had a better short game and I could get up and down from anywhere, it would not matter how consistent I am. What I need is a better short game.

I NEED A BETTER SHORT GAME

"I didn't learn how to swing a golf club until late in my career. And even though I won all those tournaments, I still struggle with consistency, and I relied on my strengths, which were hitting the ball long and high, and I could chip and putt with the best of them."

—TOM WATSON

My short game must be my problem. If I could just get up and down from everywhere, I could easily become a scratch golfer. Just watch the PGA pros, they always get up and down. They make it look so easy, even from impossible positions. The average scrambling percentage for a PGA player is 59 percent. Not as high as I thought, especially when you consider that the statistic includes balls that end up on the fringe. My guess is their scrambling percentage on these shots is well over 90 percent. Therefore, their true scrambling percentage is probably less than 50 percent. Tour pros are hitting approximately thirteen greens in regulation, again this does not include balls that land on the fringe. I am going to give them an extra hole. Therefore, they are trying to get up and down on four holes. If you get up and down 50 percent of the time and you do not have any birdies, you would be two over par. *Hmmm, I wonder if I should go back to trying to hit more greens in regulation. Why didn't anyone think of that? Oh, someone did.*

The problem with committing to having a great short game is basic economics. Most people do not have unlimited time. If you are going to allocate your efforts to where you get the biggest payback, practicing pitching and chipping is not the place. Let me explain. If you do not hit any greens in regulation and you are able to save par 50 percent of the time, you would be nine over par. However, if you could hit 50 percent of the greens in regulation and got up and down 10 percent, you would be eight over par. You are better off improving your greens in regulation (GIR). So that is where you should practice and where most people do practice. People are much smarter than I want to give them credit for.

Here is another way to look at it. If you can hit eight greens in regulation, stay away from penalty shots, and could two-putt every green, you would shoot ten over par with a 0 percent scrambling percentage. Assuming you could get to a 50 percent scrambling percentage, you would shoot five over par. That's a substantial improvement, but a long way from scratch. Assuming that you will not exceed what the PGA professionals are doing, the best way to become a scratch golfer is to improve your greens in regulation and your strokes gained putting.

With all that said, I know I have to have a good short game to become a scratch golfer. One or two shots a round is a lot. It is not that easy to get birdies to make up for a bogey. The PGA pros just do not make a lot of bogeys. You must get the ball on the green and close enough to have a reasonable chance to make par. That means you must be inside ten feet. The percentage of putts made from outside ten feet is well under 50 percent. The percentage between five and ten feet is 55 percent for the PGA. I am betting that my putting percentage is less. You also must hit it close enough to avoid three-putting. I have a friend who struggles with chipping, and the ability to pitch is not even in his playbook. He is easily giving four to five shots away every round. Maybe that is why he is an eighteen handicap.

If you miss the green, thereby hurting your GIR stat, you would still like to make par or even a birdie every so often. If the PGA professionals have a 59 percent scrambling percentage, the chance of you making par is less than 50 percent, significantly less. Your odds improve if your ball is on the fringe and you are putting to the hole, but we are not counting these situations. Your ability to scramble is dramatically affected by how bad your second shot is. If you are constantly in bunkers, in the heavy rough, twenty to forty yards away, and so on, your percentage is going to be a lot lower.

The short game is made up of three different components. First is putting. Second is chipping and pitching. Third is bunker play. I decide that my putting is okay, but I need work on the other areas. I combine chipping and pitching into the same category, because I never really understood the difference between the two. Then again, I never figured out how to hit a seven- or eight-iron around the green, either. Great chippers do this all the time. My bunker play is pathetic. I only get up and down from the bunker 10 percent of the time. More times than I would like to think about, I have left a shot in the bunker or hit it over the green, now bringing in a double bogey. Golf is such a cruel game. My goal is to hit all these shots to within ten feet of the hole. Assuming I can make 70 percent of these (slightly less than the PGA pros), I should be doing pretty well.

Okay, so here we go again. What should I do to improve my pitching and chipping game?

- Buy some new wedges—this is always guaranteed to solve your issues.

- Take some lessons or watch some short-game videos. Knowledge is key.

- Practice—now that is a strategy to consider.

- Get a shrink.

Buy some new wedges

Buying new clubs will always be the first answer. It never works, but it just seems so simple. Hope is eternal. There are companies that promote with their wedges; you are guaranteed to knock it close every time. There are also clubs called chippers. These clubs are built so they seem like a putter; however, they have a higher degree of loft. Basically, you just putt it, and it acts like a chip. Here is the problem: Most people are not good putters either, so it does not really help. There are numerous sand wedges that have such a big bounce on them that you can never miss a bunker shot. I must be honest, I have never seriously tried any of these clubs. The few times I have hit them, I cannot tell the difference. I also do not like the idea of eliminating a club just because I cannot learn to chip or hit a bunker shot with a regular club. So, I carry on with tradition. No crazy wedges for me.

Take some lessons or watch some short-game videos

This is a logical step. Learn from the experts about how to hit these shots. I decided I needed to go to the best. I signed up for the Dave Pelz three-day course. I was very excited. I flew to San Diego, and my life was going to change. I arrived at the airport, and my clubs did not show up. They were on their way to some destination but not San Diego. I was freaking out. I lost all sense of reality. I was yelling at my wife, for what reason I do not know. The school did not start until the next day, so there was hope. What do you know? The clubs showed up. Anyone in their right mind knew that they would. I was obviously not in my right mind. Okay, I am now good. Off to the class.

My grade on the three-day class was a C. It seemed like they were more interested in collecting data than they were in teaching me how to be a great short-game player. I did learn that I did not have a great short game, but I already knew that. My wife still has not forgiven me for yelling at her. The whole thing seemed like a good idea. Sigh!

Now what? I know, I need a private lesson. Stan Utley, who is considered one of the best short-game players who ever played, gives private lessons. Great, I will book him for a half day. My lesson starts at 1:00. I have a morning flight, with plenty of time to get there. I arrived at the airport, and they cancelled my flight. *Oh my god, what am I going to do?* Utley is in Phoenix. There are no flights that would get me there in time, but I could take a flight to Los Angeles and then back to Phoenix. I took it, and I was an hour late to my lesson. I was starting to think that flying to a lesson is not a good idea. I met Stan, and he was really a nice guy. He took me through a lot of different shots. Not to complain, but Stan seemed more interested in showing me how good his short game was. It was phenomenal, but I'm not sure how that helped me. In reality, I didn't learn a lot. Once again, a one-and-done experience. My ability to replicate what I learned was limited and short-lived. I never did learn to hit a bunker shot. Stan gave up on me after about a half an hour of hitting a lot of bad bunker shots. He just shook his head. He was probably thinking, *Just do not hit it in the bunkers, and you will be okay.*

I then decided to go to short-game videos. There are a lot of different videos. The problem is, they are also so basic they really are not that helpful. I am starting to think that no one really understands what they are doing, or it is impossible to explain how to improve the short game in a manner that makes sense to me. In reality, the short game is simple. However, I need to make difficult. *I wonder why?*

Practice

Practice. Why would practice help? Logically, it seems like hitting a good chip or pitch shot should not be that difficult. However, it is boring as hell to practice. Hitting seven-irons, drivers, or wedges is so much fun, and can make or break your round. If you are happy with being a ten-plus handicap, you do not need much of a short game. If you miss a green, without a good short game, you will get up and down 10 percent of the time. So, if you are hitting less than 50 percent of the greens in regulation, you will bogey eight to nine holes. I have already gone through the economics, so there is no reason to repeat myself.

However, I want to be a scratch golfer, not a ten handicap. I must commit to working on my short game. I will allocate time to practice. My plan is that when I get to the course, I will go straight to the range. I will work on my short game after I hit a few balls. I start hitting balls, and I either do not like how I am swinging, or I love how I am hitting. It doesn't really matter; I keep hitting balls. I then realize that I have only ten minutes until my tee time. I go to the short-game practice area and hit ten chips and pitches. I may even have time to hit a few bunker shots. Okay, there is my practice. The driving range is full of people, but the chipping and pitching green is completely open. We are all doing the same thing. Economics.

Why do the pros have such great short games? Maybe it is because they practice it? I heard an interesting story from a journeymen PGA pro. He said that when you are on tour, golf is your job. Assuming you are working at it nine to ten hours a day, how do you allocate your time? Let's say a practice round is five hours. You can only hit balls for so long, or you will wear yourself out. Let's say two hours. We are now at seven hours. That leaves two to four hours a day to chip, pitch, and putt. If you spend this much time every day for a couple of years, with the proper technique, you start getting pretty good.

Most of us are lucky to hit ten to twenty pitch and chip shots a week, and about that many putts. Let's not even talk about technique. I think you know the answer about why most people's short games—including mine—are not that great. I need to stop complaining about it.

Get a shrink

Chipping and pitching are not difficult shots. What makes them difficult, besides lack of complete talent and lack of practice, is our heads. Chipping and pitching are more of a head game than anything else, except for putting. Just wait until I get to putting. I really cannot afford a golf shrink, but I can read. Once again, there are numerous books about getting your mind right. Dr. Rotella has made a fortune on his golf psychology books. There are lots of books, and I will go through them in more detail when I get to the mental game. However, I cannot tell you how many times I have stood over a straight chip shot and let my mind take over. This means I have entered the world of fear. What exactly I am afraid of, I am not sure. But hey, this is important stuff. I then proceed to hit the ball thin, sending it across the green, or fat, so it does not go anywhere. How embarrassing. I am sure that everyone is laughing at me. I either lower my head in shame or yell some sort of profanity, so everyone knows that I did not find that shot acceptable. The truth is, no one cares, unless you are their partner. Even then, they just feel badly for you. They have done the same thing themselves, many times.

Everyone says, "Stop being afraid, just hit the ball." However, this fear thing must be real. I know great golfers who have gotten the chipping yips and now chip one-handed. I know another guy who carries another club in this free hand. I thought that looked illegal, but it isn't. It seems like an aid to me, but hey, what do I know?

I wonder if you noticed that I did not have get into decent shape in the list for how to improve my short game. That is the one thing about the short game: being physically in great shape isn't a critical component, except for bunker play, where being able to generate a lot of speed is very helpful. They say that this is one of the reasons that men are better bunker players than women. Men swing faster. I am not sure if that is true or not. However, who am I to question them.

An excuse for not practicing—it really is not my fault

I have talked about really working on my short game for more than forty years. The truth, my short-game practice is less than 10 percent of my full-swing practice. Why don't I practice it more? The problem is, there are no good places to practice. Most golf courses have limited practice areas for the short game. There are a limited number of shots you can hit, and there is never enough room to simulate what you are going to see on the golf course. I found the best way to practice is to go out on the course when there is limited play and hit five or six shots each on the various greens. This gives me a more realistic sense as how to hit different shots. What a great idea! I bet I have done it twenty times over forty years. Does that qualify?

I said that my putting was okay. I think I was wrong.

IF ONLY I COULD PUTT

"A 'gimme' can best be defined as an agreement between two golfers, neither of who can putt very well."

—UNKNOWN

As I am watching this guy make putt after putt after putt while I am missing putt after putt after putt, I tell myself, *If I could putt like this guy, I could become a scratch golfer*. I hit a ball within five feet of the hole. An easy birdie, but I miss it. I always miss these putts. I am standing over a two-foot putt. All I can think is, *Do not miss it*. I do not think this is the right thought.

Okay, so what do I need to do to improve my putting. I bet you can guess.

- Buy a new putter—the easiest solution.

- Change my putting style and grip—the pros keep changing their grips.

- Get a putting lesson. Who takes a putting lesson?

- Watch some putting videos or read a book—knowledge can't hurt, can it?

Before I get into all the different things I have done, I want to put some prospective into putting.

The simplest stroke in golf is putting. Although it is the simplest stroke, it seems to be the most frustrating. Putting is the only time in golf that when you miss, there is no doubt that you are adding another stroke to your score. Every other shot—except if you hit it out of bounds or into a water hazard—you believe you have a chance to recover and still make par, or even a birdie. Additionally, if you miss a short putt, your mind tells you that everyone around you is laughing at you. When people laugh at you, your fight-or-flight mechanism kicks in and your survival is at stake. Over time, you are so nervous hitting a two-foot putt that you start missing them. Then you get the yips. The yips are not a good thing. Believe it or not, there are books written about eliminating the yips. The reality is that no one is laughing at you. They are glad they didn't have to try to make that putt. They have a lot of empathy for you.

Strangely, putting is the only stroke where everyone says having your own style is acceptable. I have never really understood this. It seems like there should be some science on the best way to take a club back six to twelve inches, then hit the ball with a square face. Putting is no more difficult than that. Now, there is also the subject of how hard to hit a putt and how the green is going to break. Still, it really is not that hard to hit it close. Hmmm, the problem is that close is not good enough. It needs to go in that four-and-a-quarter-inch cup. It is kind of small, especially if it is sitting thirty feet away with varying slopes and speeds. Okay, it is hard. When you think about it, it is amazing how close we hit it to the hole.

If your GIR is 100 percent and you shoot par, you will have thirty-six putts. This represents half of your shots on a par-seventy-two course. Because of the sheer number of putts, it obviously creates one of the biggest places to add to or subtract from your score. Your first putt on each hole is by far the most difficult because of distance. Typically, your second putt is going to be less than three feet. The pros make one inch to three-foot putts 96 percent of the time. You will make fewer unless you get the yips. Then your rate goes down to less than 50 percent. Remember, the yips are not a good thing. I know, I had them. Emphasis on the "had."

I decided to look at the PGA pro's putting average, and I am some surprised how few putts they are making from twenty to twenty-five feet. In case you are wondering, it is about 12 percent. If they hit it within five to ten feet, the percentage goes up to 55 percent, which is still not as high as you might think. Valerie Hogan told Ben Hogan at the 1937 Los Angeles Open, "If you want to make more putts, hit it closer to the hole." Well said.

I have done a lot of research on putting. During this comprehensive research, I came across a brilliant concept by Geoff Mangrum in his book *Ultimate Golf*. It is more than 250 pages about putting. Can you imagine writing a book about taking a club back six to twelve inches and hitting a ball into a hole for more than 250 pages? Pelz wrote a similar book on putting that was 385 pages. The sad part is, I have read both books. I am still not a great putter. I gave someone Pelz's book, and it ruined him for life. He has never been able to putt since.

In Mangrum's book, he states that we are gravity machines. What does that mean? Your subconscious understands gravity. If it did not, you could not survive. No land animal could. You can walk, run, and jump because you understand gravity. You can throw a ball a certain distance and you are able to catch a ball coming out of the sky because you understand gravity. You can ride a bicycle or a skateboard because you understand gravity. You can hit a baseball or play tennis because you understand gravity. It takes a little bit of time to understand how gravity affects something. Watch a young child learning to catch a ball. Initially they struggle, but it does not take long before they can easily catch a ball. If you practice, you continue to get better at understanding gravity. It is your subconscious mind that is getting better. Your conscious mind has no concept of gravity. However, your ego resides in your conscious mind, so it is constantly trying to tell your subconscious mind what to do. It is not working for most of us. Okay, it doesn't work for anyone.

Since your conscious mind does not understand gravity, why would you ever bring your conscious mind into play when putting? If you are, stop it. This includes green reading. Your subconscious is much better at reading greens than your conscious mind. That is why you hear that your first read is always the best. To emphasize this point, I cannot remember how many times I have told myself, *This putt is uphill, so I need to hit it harder.* You do hit it harder, but it tends to go way past the whole. My subconscious knows how hard to hit the ball. I need to let it. *Famous last words.*

Another example is how many times have I hit a long putt that I knew was going in the hole, and it does. When I get this feeling, my guess is that more than 95 percent of the time, it does go in. Why? My subconscious knows that it is going in because it understands gravity.

You do have to train your subconscious if you want to be a great putter. That means you need to practice hitting putts from various distances. When you practice, let your subconscious take over. Don't think about distance, or whether the putt is uphill or downhill. Let your subconscious learn. It will. When you take it to the course, you need to trust yourself. You need to pick your line and trust it. You will be pleasantly surprised.

Last, if you can get your distance right and you can hit your putt where you intend to, then you need to be able to read the green. Amazingly, since we are gravity machines, we can also read greens with a fair amount of accuracy. Remember the cup is only four-and-a-quarter inches, and there is a bumpy surface between you and the hole. The odds are stacked against you.

So why is the cup four-and-a-quarter inches? The size of the current hole was first established in 1829 by the Royal Musselburgh Golf Club in Scotland. They built a hole cutter that is still used today. We all talk about Saint Andrews being the home of golf, but Royal Musselburgh had all the best golfers until the Morrises started playing golf. It was not until 1891 that the Royal and Ancient Golf Club determined that the diameter of the hole should be four-and-a-quarter inches. Before that, each club determined what size of hole they wanted. My guess is the greens keeper at Royal Musselburgh sold his hole cutter, and that diameter became the standard. It just took the R&A a long time to catch up.

Okay, I digressed a bit, but it was fun. Well, maybe not that fun. Let's get on to how I have tried to improve my putting.

Buy a new putter

Again, this should always be the first choice. It is just so much easier than any other option. I have only owned ten to fifteen different putters over my forty years of playing. I know a guy who is a good putter who has more than hundred putters. Arnold Palmer had more than a thousand. Dustin Johnson changes putters all the time. Getting a new putter is one of the most common fixes for bad putting.

Putting is a head game, so buying a new putter makes perfect sense. It gives you a whole new sense of confidence. I knew a guy who carried two putters. If he missed a putt with one of the putters, the other one came out. I remember the first time he started to do this. I was watching him and realized that he had a different putter. I was shocked and thought to myself, *This is not right.* I asked him how many clubs he had. He said fourteen; he just removed his three-iron. He could not hit that either.

I wonder if buying a new putter is the answer. No one gets their putter custom fit for them; they just buy them off the shelf. They would never do that with their other clubs. That's the answer. You need to have your putter custom fit for you. Being a PXG guy, I ran up to PXG's world headquarters to get fitted. I spent over an hour trying different putters, and I found the perfect putter. At least that is what their machine said. Who am I to question their machine? I was rolling the ball perfectly. I was set. I should cut at least four or five shots off my score. Same story, I went out to play, and I was still missing putts. Another three hundred dollars lost. Okay, I did keep using the putter, so all was not lost.

Change your putting style and grip

When I first started playing, everyone putted using a conventional grip and a square or slightly open stance. Then left-hand low came into existence. Next was the long putter, then the belly putter. The golf authorities, after thirty years, decided that anchoring a putter was no longer legal, effectively eliminating the long and belly putters since what made them work was anchoring the club. However, they have now manipulated how to use the belly putter. It is now an arm putter; at least that is what I call it. Currently, there are so many acceptable putting styles and grips that you could not ever list them all. The biggest changes are with the grip. There is left-hand low (used to be called cross-handed, but there is nothing cross-handed about it), the claw, pencil grip, modified pencil, and so on. Sergio Garcia won a tournament putting with his eyes closed. Lexi Thompson also closes her eyes, but that didn't help her in the 2021 US Open. Jordan Spieth used to look at the hole, now he doesn't. He was one of the best putterin the world, and he changed.

I was a conventional putter and would say I was a good putter. When I moved to Arizona and the courses, I played on had hard fast greens that were a little tricky, and I got the yips. My world came to an end. I could not make a one-foot putt. The yips are the strangest thing ever. I went out and practiced and made hundred three-foot putts in a row. Whenever I had a short putt on the course, my whole body would just flinch. The yips have caused many great players to quit the game. I learned that your mind, once wired, does not forget. The only way to get rid of the yips is to change something in your putting. I have putted with my eyes closed, looking at the hole, and finally settled on left-hand low. *So far, so good.*

I have a friend who was going through the same thing and told him that he had to change something about his putting. He said there is no way he needed to change. A year later, he is using the claw and now putts great. Unfortunately, he spent a year hating the game.

Even after five years, when I try to go conventional, the yips come back after two or three short putts. Crazy stuff.

Take a putting lesson

I do not really believe that the cure is getting another new putter. Plus, the pocketbook was saying that was not a good idea. I decided that I should take a putting lesson. I have never taken a putting lesson. I do not think most PGA pros like to give putting lessons. I do not know a lot of people who have ever had a true putting lesson. Maybe that is the reason very few people can putt. I decide to sign up for a putting lesson.

I show up to the lesson with my putter in hand and three golf balls. I bet 90 percent of golfers, when they practice putting, putt with three golf balls. I have no idea why. We all drop three balls and hit to the same hole and then, after missing all of them, do it again. Over and over again. They say this is bad practice. We are teaching ourselves to miss putts. Let's not bring science into the equation.

My teacher tells me to hit some putts and I do. I hit three. My instructor said that my alignment sucked. Really! That is it. I guess it is hard to make a putt if you aren't aligned right. I fixed my alignment, and I did start putting better. Not great but better. However, once I was on the course, where everything is changing, my alignment went off. I worked on it, but I did not see dramatic improvement. I decide that my alignment is fixed, so there must be another problem. The pro did not make any other suggestions. I guess there not much to say about a twelve-inch stroke.

The problem must be my green reading. Who can teach me to read a green?

Watch a video or read a book

I think that the reason most teaching pros are teaching and not playing is because they cannot putt. I had the opportunity to play with Chuck Quintin of Rotary Golf, and he had the best swing I have ever seen, by far. However, his putting is not so great. I do not think asking a teaching pro how to putt is the right answer. The answer must be in a book or a video.

To read a green, they say that you should look for the high point and putt to that high point. I am never sure where the high point really is. I can guess, but that does not seem very precise. Both Mangrum and Pelz, who are self-acclaimed experts in putting, would tell you that when you use this method, you will hit the ball on the low side. They go through a calculation on how to determine where to hit the ball. When I read either Mangrum's or Pelz's book, my mind starts to fog over. I guess that after 250 pages and 385 pages of reading, I can forgive myself. The problem is that they are talking to your conscious mind. My conscious mind cannot putt.

There is a great concept called Aim Point. Aim Point is about feeling how much the putt is going to break by using your feet. The theory is that your eyes can be easily fooled, so you cannot trust what you are seeing. Using Aim Point, you feel the slope of the green by standing at various positions between your ball and the hole, depending on the length of the putt to determine what is the slope percentage is. Once you determine the slope percentage, you stand behind the ball and put up the number of fingers you felt the slope was. If you feel 2 percent, you put up two fingers and putt to that point where the outside of your finger is. This is a quite simple explanation, and while it has a lot of good aspects to it, there are still a lot of variables to make it precise. The one thing I noticed was what I thought was the high point was too low. *Hmmm. I think it is something I should try. Can't hurt.*

Last is the plum bobbing. Plum bobbing is about as accurate as weather forecasting, but it does give you a general idea. Aim Point would say that if you are going to plum bob, you should hang the club from your thorax and see which way the club goes. The ability to manipulate the golf club is too great when you are holding your hand extended from your body. However, the problem with plum bobbing is the slope of a green is rarely more than 2 or 3 percent. Do you really think you can tell the difference between 2 percent and 3 percent? I am guessing not.

Regardless, if you do not hit it the right direction, the possibility of making a putt is pretty low. However, I have made some putts where I was aiming one way and I either pulled or pushed the ball right into the hole. There is a saying that even a broken clock is right twice a day. However, that is not the best way to putt. Another theory is that my subconscious just took over and forced me to hit it in the right spot. I like that theory. *Just trust my subconscious.* My conscious mind is yelling at me, "No, trust me."

Assuming your putt is hit in the right direction and with the right speed, it still does not mean that it is going to go in. The greens have a significant amount of variation in the grass, bumps, footprints, and so on. Have you ever played in the late evening and seen all the footprints and imperfections on the green? You wonder how you make anything. Dave Pelz did a study where he took a true roller and for a fifteen-foot putt was only able to make eight out of ten putts. A true roller ensures that the ball is rolled on the exact same line at the exact same speed. If you only make 80 percent of the putts under these circumstances, how many putts do you think you can make without it? You see why the pros are only making 12 percent of putts between twenty and twenty-five feet.

One last question I always ask myself is, *How far past the hole you should be trying to hit it?* Mangrum did an amazing analysis on this very subject. He calculated where the ball would hit in the cup based on the number of revolutions per second the ball is rolling when it gets to the cup. The following is the chart with the corresponding distance past the cup. The cup has a four-and-a-quarter-inch diameter. One revolution per second (rps) is equal to 5.3 inches. This analysis presumes you hit the ball into the center of the cup. Since most putts are breaking, the cup gets smaller the harder you hit the ball. A 1-rps putt utilizes all four-and-a-quarter inches. An 8-rps putt only uses 1.68 inches, the diameter of the ball.

RPS	Distance Past Hole Center Cut	Mr. Mangrum's Analysis
1	1.05 inches	A 1-rps putt drops in front of the front wall and hits in front of the center of the hole
2	6.35 inches	A 2-rps putt hits the bottom dead center
3	11.65 inches	A 3-rps putt never hits the back wall, but hits beyond the center of the bottom
4	16.95 inches	A 4-rps putt hits the point where the bottom of the cup and the back wall starts
5	22.5 inches	A 5-rps putt hits the bottom of the back wall
6	27.55 inches	A 6-rps putt hits near the center of the back wall
7	32.85 inches	A 7-rps putt hits near the top of the cup liner
8	38.15 inches	An 8-rps putt will hit about half an inch below the rim

Mr. Pelz said that your putt should go eighteen inches beyond the cup, which would be somewhere between seventeen and twenty-two inches at 4 and 5 rps. Mr. Mangrum would disagree. Mr. Pelz would be right if you hit every putt center cut. However, we do not hit putts center cut. We are usually slightly outside center cut. Mr. Mangrum says that for slightly outside center cut putts, you should take his analysis and double it. Therefore, a 3-rps putt acts more like a 6-rps putt. He believes that a 2-rps is optimal. Under his theory, this is a 4-rps putt, which equates to what Pelz was saying. The one thing that becomes obvious is that when people try to ram the ball to the back of the hole, they bring a lot of risk into play if they were to miss.

While this is great fun, it does not make me a better putter. I am not trying to bang the ball three feet past the hole. *I am good with a six-to-twelve-inch second putt. Wait, how many times do I even hit my first putt past the hole?* I should know this number, but it would take some effort to track it. Who has time to do that? I start watching people putt, and

I notice that people leave a lot more putts short than they do long. I started watching myself as well. I leave a lot of putts short. I wonder why a three-foot putt that went short is better than a three-foot putt that went long. Our minds, or I should say my mind, does not like hitting a putt long. I watch the pros putt; they rarely leave a putt short. Hmmm. I came up with a brilliant fact. Bet as much money as you can on this statement. Short putts do not go in. There, I said it. Why do I hit putts short?

I need a strategy. First, I need to get more realistic about how many putts I am going to make. Why will this make me a better putter? Because I need to stop stressing out when a putt does not go in. More importantly, I need to stop trying to make unneeded changes that are hurting me more than helping me. I am not allowing my subconscious to practice. My new putting thought gets me to practice for a couple of weeks, then I am on to something else.

Next, I need to hit my first putt, so I have an easy second putt. Three putts are costly, not only to my score but to my mind. I hate three-putting. It can truly ruin your momentum. Hitting it closer to the hole is usually more about distance than direction. If you do not do either well, you are not realizing how strong of a gravity machine you are. Your subconscious mind is listening to your conscious mind, even when your conscious mind has no idea what it is doing. As long as you aren't hurting yourself, the subconscious mind really doesn't care that much, so it will listen.

In conclusion, I need to walk up to my putt, look at where I am trying to hit the ball, and just hit it. So easy to say. Not so easy to execute.

The best player in the world is Jack Nicklaus. He was also considered the best game manager. Maybe that is the answer, better game management.

BETTER GAME MANAGEMENT MUST BE THE ANSWER

"Success depends almost entirely on how effectively you learn to manage the game's two ultimate adversaries: the course and yourself."

—JACK NICKLAUS

Better game management? *Hmmm, I need to think about that. That's it. That is the problem.* I wonder if you asked the best PGA players what game management means to them if you would get some vague answer. My guess is you would. I know the pros do things that few amateurs do. First, they do have a specific plan on where they are going to hit the ball. They have an advantage, because they are told where all the pins are going to be placed, which allows them to plan where they want to hit their second shot from. They have a book that tells them how the green is going to break. Not sure why we amateurs do not do the same thing. I guess we just know better than they do. This year, they limited the type of green reading book you can have. Only annotations made from the naked eye can be used. Yet they are still using them. Game management is much more than just planning out your shots. It is your ability to react when you have shots that you did not plan out. Are you conservative or a gambler? Most of us have no business being a gambler; however, most amateurs are much bigger gamblers than any PGA pro would ever think of being. Here are four stories about incredibly bad game management.

- There is a saying that you should never follow up a bad shot with a stupid shot. You can tell I learned that lesson well. During the first round of the Fox Hill Club Championship, my gambling obsession kicked in. I tried to fight the urge, but I gave in. On the fourteenth hole, a par five, I hit the ball left and the ball ended up behind a little tree. Right behind that tree was a bigger tree. My only logical shot was to chip it out and hit it on to the fairway. If I hit this shot, I could have technically gotten to the green from there, but worst case I would have had a short pitch shot and still a 30 to 40 percent chance to save par. The gambler inside me said, *You can cut this ball fifty to sixty yards and have an easy shot to the green.* The ball did not cut. I lucked out because the ball went through all the trees, almost on to the fifteenth fairway. My gambler was not done. I then had three options: pitch it straight back onto the fairway with a long fourth shot to the green, play down fifteen and have a sixty- to seventy-yard shot to the green (par was still possible), or hit the ball through an opening where the pin was staring directly at me. I had a ten-foot window, plenty of room. Guess which shot I took? I was shocked that I hit a tree and it came right back at me. Now I had no choice, and I hit it back onto the fairway. I then had an easy fifty-yard shot to the pin, and my mind is saying I must try to make six. I hit the next shot right at the flag, but for some reason, it went long and ended up in some really thick rough. I tried to hit a perfect shot so I could make six, but the rough was so thick I ended up leaving it in the rough. Then I chipped it long and missed the putt. An easy nine. You usually do not win a club championship when you take a nine. The sad part is, on eighteen, I did the same thing. I hit it in the trees, but thought I could hit a cut shot up and over some trees from 208 yards out. I hit a good shot, but it just caught the top of the tree, which knocked it straight down. I now had a ninety-yard shot to the hole, which I left in the sand trap right up against the bank. I took a nice seven.

- At the Columbine Member Guest, my gambler again took over. We won our flight, and we were on the second hole of the horse race. My partner hit it into the trees, and I had two options. I could either chip it out, giving my partner a 120-yard shot to the green, or I could hit it under the trees, over the sand bunker, and onto the green. Even though my partner pleaded with me to chip it out, my gambler said I got this shot. I had a five-iron in my hand, but decided to use my four-hybrid. I hit the shot perfectly, and the ball hit the green on the fly. Unfortunately, it was still going hundred miles an hour. It bounced hard and flew into the river that is thirty yards off the green. We were out of the tournament. We had a chance to make par, and a bogey would have gotten us into a chip off. It was a costly mistake.

- I was in a tournament and one of the guys I played with hit the ball into a hazard, but he could theoretically hit the ball. He was playing well and was in the hunt. The ball was about ten yards off the green, and his ball was surrounded by a bunch of weeds. The only way he could hit the ball was back-handed or left-handed. He was not able to take any kind of swing at it. The logical play was to take a penalty drop. At worst, he would take a six, a double bogey, but he had a real opportunity to get up and down for a bogey five. He decided to hit the ball left-handed. My guess is that he does not practice a lot of left-handed shots from the weeds from a hazard. I could be wrong. He ended up grounding his club trying to hit the shot (a two-shot penalty back then) and never got it out of the weeds. He ended up taking a nine on the hole and missed the cut by three shots.

- The last example is more understandable. The guy ended up with a straight downhill lie (probably forty-five degrees) next to a bunker in grass that had to be eight inches high. We could hardly see the ball, and it was an impossible shot. He had two realistic options. First, he could try to hit the ball, which he did, or he could have called the ball unplayable. If he elected this option, he could take the ball back as far as he wanted on the line between his ball and the flag and drop the ball in a place where the ball was hittable. He ended up taking an eight on the hole instead of a probable six and missed the cut by one shot.

When I thought about these examples, it seems that whenever we feel like we can hit the ball, we go ahead and hit it. I have seen very few people (typically good golfers) who take a drop. We act like a penalty shot is ten shots instead of just one. It does not make sense that we will not just take a penalty shot. After doing some research, studies have concluded that taking a penalty shot is similar to receiving a punishment. I then researched avoiding punishments and discovered an interesting phenomenon. Avoiding a punishment is like receiving a reward. If you avoid a punishment, your mind views it the same as receiving a reward for doing something right. So, when faced with taking a penalty shot (a punishment) or trying to hit the shot, a person is naturally inclined to attempt to hit the shot even if he 100 percent knows that the outcome will be much worse. The human mind views failure much differently than a punishment. Getting a reward for avoiding a punishment is much more important than failing. It makes us happy. Then we go to the next hole and reality sets in. Now we are not happy.

I know this, but I still rarely take the logical penalty shot. I will admit that since I have been playing in the desert, I take a lot more penalty shots. Those cactuses hurt. Maybe the answer is to change the terminology in my head from a penalty shot to something like taking an additional shot. Who knows, but if I continue to think about it as a punishment, the chances of me shaking my head in disbelief with the next shot I hit is pretty high.

The concept of game management eludes me. There is not a lot written about game management. What I have read is basic. For some reason, they cannot predict what is going on in my mind. I think I live my life logically, just not in golf. My concept on game management is to hit it as far as I can, aim at every pin, and then go conservative and leave 80 percent of my putts short. I wonder why we get conservative on putting and chipping. I guess our fear mechanism takes over at this time, because we know that missing a putt costs us a stroke. It is the only time we look at it that way. I think I can always recover when I am not on the putting green.

Logically, game management is not that difficult. All I need to do is build the foundation to make sure I manage to optimize my performance on the golf course. Sounds like I went to MBA school. The basics are simple.

- Develop a plan on how to play the course. Plan where I am going to hit the ball, what club am I going to use, and so on.

- Develop a contingency plan when I do not hit the shot I planned. How am I going to play when I am in trouble? What amount of risk am I willing to take, and when does my risk profile change?

- Realistically know how far I hit my clubs, both carry and roll. Carry is more important, because you need to know if you can carry the trouble that may be in front of you. I think I hit my clubs farther than I do. For some reason, if I hit a hit a seven-iron 175 yards one time, that is my new distance. Even twenty years later. Sadly, my mean was probably 160 and declining every year. Those fifteen yards put a lot of balls in the bunker or in the water.

- Stop shooting at every pin. Johnny Miller wrote about developing a red, yellow, and green-light approach. To make this approach work, I need to have a good understanding of my basic shot pattern. How far right, left, long do I hit shots? My mind thinks I hit them all right at the pin. Once you understand this, you can then play better shots to the green.

- Do not intentionally bring trouble into play. If there is an out-of-bounds or a water hazard, I should make sure that I do not hit a shot that brings it into play. That thought seldom crosses my mind.

- Use the 80-percent rule. Don't hit a shot unless there is an 80 percent chance or better that you will pull it off. Thinking about it, since I overestimate my abilities, I should make it 90 percent.

These are all good thoughts to remember when I am done playing and evaluating my score and what went wrong.

When I think about my game management, I realize that I have lost my ability to think logically. When I hit a shot and it turns out to be long, I instantly think to myself, *I hit too much club.* I have suddenly gotten longer. Amazing how that happened. I believe myself and go down a club the next time I have that same distance. Interestingly, I start hitting numerous shots short. I tell myself that the ball is coming up short because I just did not catch it. Unfortunately, it always takes a while to recalibrate. Sometimes, I never do. It just depends. On what? I have no idea. I also do the same thing in putting. I just do not want to go long. This makes even less sense because a short putt never goes in. *Hmmm, the same is true for any shot to the green.*

Common sense would say that at least 80 percent of your shots should be slightly long. You will tend to take trouble out of play. The designers put the trouble in front of the green. They know who we are. Going slightly long also gives you the best opportunity to make that one in hundred shot and holing it out. Yet, a lot of people would argue this theory because most greens slope back to forward, so we do not want a downhill putt. This is true, but the severity of slope and the speed of the greens are rarely enough to justify this logic. We are not playing Augusta National. There may be one or at the most two greens on your course where you should be short. However, I seem to like hitting out of bunkers and dropping from water hazards, so I play it short.

I want to hit the ball farther. It is not just my ego talking, I know that by hitting the ball farther I will be closer to the green. It is much easier to hit a wedge close to the pin than a seven-iron. However, what amazes me is how often I am willing to hit a longer club right into the teeth of trouble. Does the extra ten to thirty yards increase my chance to make a birdie enough to risk the chance of bringing a double bogey into play? One day, I was playing a par five and hit a good drive. The wind was in my face, and there was no way I could reach the green in two. There is a lake to the left that starts at about 120 yards from the green and goes all the way up to the green. The fairway is right of the green and is probably twenty-five to thirty yards wide. I decided to hit a five-iron instead of a seven-iron to give me another thirty yards. The seven-iron would have left me 130 yards from the green, while the five-iron would leave me hundred yards from the green. Shockingly, I hit the ball slightly left, and it went into the water. The moment after it went into the water, I knew I should have hit a seven-iron. For some reason, I just needed the extra thirty yards. Now I know that everyone reading this will say they would have hit the seven-iron. My guess is that most of you would have hit a five-iron or even a bigger club, thinking you could get to the green. I have seen it too many times.

I decided to look at this dilemma objectively. Let's assume that on average, my five-iron goes ten yards right or left of my intended target. Without going into a standard deviation calculation, ten yards becomes closer to thirty yards if you want to be 99 percent sure where your shot will go. The fairway is thirty yards wide, and I was aiming slightly to the right, giving me twenty yards of error. The odds of me hitting it left are around 15 percent. If I had hit a seven-iron, there was zero chance of it going into the water. Now let's look at the other side. How much closer to the pin will I hit a hundred-yard shot compared to a 130-yard shot? I do not have the exact data, which I should, but I am going to assume that on average, I will hit the ball ten feet to fifteen feet closer with a hundred-yard shot. On average, I hit a hundred-yard shot ten to twenty-five feet from the pin. The PGA professionals make 38 percent of their ten-footers, 22 percent of their fifteen-footers, 14 percent of their twenty-footers, and 10 percent of their twenty-five-footers. Last I checked I am not a PGA professional, so I am assuming I am 70 percent as good as they are. Doing the math, the additional thirty yards increased my chance of making a birdie by less than 3 percent. Not a great trade-off.

The reality is that I did not need to do all of this analysis to know what the right answer was. Yet, I still hit the shot. It's like going to Vegas and thinking you are going to consistently win. The odds are against you, and eventually, the odds always win.

We all know that good game management can save numerous shots and will make you a more consistent player. However, very few people execute a good game management strategy. We must feel that executing a good game-management plan will limit our ability to have a great round. Let's be honest, hitting a homerun in baseball is much more fun than hitting a bunch of singles.

I wonder if I am going to change. Maybe I will, when I decide that it is more important to be a consistently good golfer and stop trying to shoot that record round. The funny part is the odds are better that I will shoot the record round when I am playing within my abilities.

You know, before thinking about game management, I should work on my mental game.

WHAT I NEED IS A BETTER MENTAL GAME

"Good players have the power to think while they are competing. Most golfers are not thinking, even when they believe they are. They are only worrying. Rather than worry, be mindful of the shot at hand and go ahead and play it as if you are going to hit the best shot of your life. You really might do it."

—HARVEY PENICK

How many books say that golf is more about the six inches between your ears than anything else? A good friend of mine keeps saying that the only thing keeping me from being a scratch golfer is my mind. I wonder what he is trying to tell me. It doesn't sound very nice.

Okay, how do I prove him wrong? I mean, I have a mind like a steel trap. I always have it together on the course. I meditate every day; my mind is strong. I am at peace with the world. I then came up with an idea to prove him wrong. I need to separate my swing handicap from my mind handicap. This is based on the belief that they are independent of each other. I am calling my swing handicap my capability handicap. The second is my mind handicap.

My capability handicap is what I could practically score with my current swing and short game, taking out the effects of lack of focus, lack of knowledge, poor judgment, tension, and so on. The mind handicap is how many strokes result because of my failure in one or more of these areas. I calculated my mind handicap by taking the difference between my capability handicap and my current handicap.

The first step was to figure out how to determine a capability handicap. I decided that if I played a two-ball scramble, this would give me a reasonable capability handicap. A two-ball scramble is where you hit two balls on every shot. You take the best shot and then hit it again until you hole out. My theory is, your swing is not changing shot after shot, but having a second shot helps you eliminate tension and poor judgment and can create better knowledge and more focus. I played twenty rounds on four different golf courses. Surprisingly, I found that 60 to 65 percent of my best shots were my first shot. In all these rounds, I did not make any long bombs or chip anything in that I could have considered adjusting. That would be an interesting exercise. I made a couple of twenty-five-foot putts on both my first and second shots. I did not three-putt, and I did not have any penalty shots. I did not hit every green in regulation, but usually got up and down. I had a total of sixteen bogeys in twenty rounds of golf. It was an interesting experiment. I learned a lot about myself, and about my game.

I know this sounds unbelievable, but my capability handicap index was a plus four. My handicap at the time I did this test was a five. Therefore, I determined that my mind handicap was a nine. That didn't seem very good. I can tell you that if I were a plus four, I would be more than happy. I would be ecstatic. The conclusion of this test was to listen to my friend and "Stop working on [my] swing." I would start working exclusively on my mind. What a concept! However, what part of my mind is causing me problems? I think it is fear. Fear is a challenging thing to figure out.

I wonder what the differential would be for a PGA professional. My guess is their mind handicap would be fairly small. What about a high handicapper? Would their mind handicap also be smaller, because they truly need to work on their swing or short game? I tried to get some people to try it, and they just looked at me like I had lost my mind. Hmmm.

Okay, I now have a new plan. I decided to go on a ten-day silent meditation retreat to get my head right. I was coming back a scratch golfer. Okay, while I did go on a ten-day silent retreat, it was not for golf. However, while I was there, it got me thinking. I did not have much else to do. I came up with this realization.

"If I could improve my mind handicap by more than 50 percent, I would be a scratch golfer."

Okay, how do I do this? Let's start with reading sports psychology books. I have read them all. I saw a new one that just came out. It is called *Simplicity,* by Steve Yellen, and it is written for people like me who are on an infinite number of swing changes. Maybe this book has the answer. I do think it may have some of the answers, but the answer? Doubtful. I need to figure out the root cause of the issue. Here are my thoughts.

Stop time traveling

I do not believe that time travel is possible, except when I am playing golf. Okay, I lied, I time travel all the time. Let me explain. How many times when you are having a good round do you travel into the future to see the record round you just shot or how you blew up? How many times have you gone back into the past to relive a bad shot or a good shot over and over again? When sitting around the nineteenth hole, do you ever travel into the past talking about your golf tragedies? When you travel into the past, do you tend to relive your tragedies more often and with greater emotion than your good shots? Most people do, because our first instinct is survival. Back when we truly needed to worry about survival, we had to remember the terrible things that happened so we could avoid them in the future. I doubt that a bad golf shot qualifies as a survival event. Your subconscious mind does not think so.

So why do we mentally time travel? Studies have shown that we are fundamentally wired to only react to clear changes that occur in our environment. People are programmed to conserve as much energy as possible, and if we reacted to everything that was going on we could not function. Remembering past events allow us to quickly interpret changes. Unfortunately, using past events places a filter on what is happening, and we do not accurately remember what exactly happened in the past. This applies to everyone else but me. I remember everything perfectly. People also tend to use past events to predict what is going to happen in the future. Our predictions always come true because we mentally shut off the possibility of a different outcome. While I don't believe we will ever stop time traveling, what would happen if we only time traveled into possibilities we want to create?

Golf psychologists tell you not to time travel. Personally, I do not think this is possible. I would suggest the following.

1. When time traveling into the past, think about great shots. Just delete bad shots by saying to yourself, "Delete" to remove them from your memory banks. Especially important is not to put any emotion into these shots. Your mind remembers emotions, not words. A bad shot may be painful, but survival is not dependent on it. We want to use past experiences to predict future outcomes, so it only makes sense to use a good memory instead of a bad one. I am currently using a concept from the book *With Winning in Mind*, where I go through my round and just write down the good shots I have. I am doing this to remember the good shots. Don't even think about a bad shot. It is a surprisingly good exercise. Time will tell.

2. When time traveling into the future, believe that you are going to shoot a great round. Create the feeling of shooting a low score. Your mind does not know the difference between what you tell it and what is happening. So, you might as well tell your mind what is happening is great. I realize golf psychologists say to just think about the next shot, but again, people are wired to survive, so I do not think that is possible. (This is coming from someone who took psychology 101 in college.) We are trying to predict the outcome so we can live or die. I find it interesting that the better we are playing, the more we time travel. My suggestion is to make sure you are creating great possibilities. Quickly delete the bad possibilities. Again, this is easier said than done.

3. Last, get into the present when it is time to hit a shot. This is the only time you have for control over the result. This is not the time for time travel. Only focus on the type of shot you want to hit and the target you are aiming at. If you start to time travel, recognize it and refocus again on the target, then hit the shot with complete trust and confidence. Once you hit the shot, accept the outcome. If you hit a good or great shot, reward yourself. If a bad shot, quickly hit the delete button. Your subconscious remembers what you

get emotional about. Get emotional about your great shots, nothing else. Remember, whatever the outcome, it will not change your life unless it is on the eighteenth hole of the Masters.

A critical point to remember: we are built to time travel, and since it is only our mind that time travels, we might as well travel into amazing possibilities.

GETTING OUT OF YOUR COMFORT ZONE—IT IS OKAY TO GO LOW

"Golf is played in the present. If you can wash your mind clean each time while walking to your next shot, you have the makings of a champion."

—HARVEY PENICK

Harvey Penick tells a great story. A student came to visit him from out of town. He was told that Harvey could help him become a dominant amateur player. Harvey told him to go hit a bucket of balls and he would watch him. The gentleman started hitting balls, and Harvey went up to watch him. The guy was hitting balls, and he hit it like a pro. Harvey watched him for about an hour. At the end, the guy looked at him for advice, and Harvey asked him what his last two scores were. The gentleman said seventy-seven and seventy-eight.

Harvey looked at him and said, "I see only one thing wrong with your game."

The man cried out, "What is it?"

Harvey said, "Your scores are too high."

The man was beside himself. He was expecting to hear the secret. He told his friends that he thought Harvey was a fraud. The funny part of the story was the next week this gentleman went out and won his first golf tournament. Harvey concluded that he just needed someone to tell him it was all right to do it.

The reason I love this story is because I think I could score much better if I just gave myself permission to do it. I have developed stories in my head about what I can shoot. This is what everyone calls the comfort zone. Economists would call it "Regression to the Mean." This means that people will always perform at their mean. The outliers are just that, outliers. When things are going great, we move back to where we have always been. The same thing happens when things are going bad. This is the reason why people will have a great nine and follow it up with a bad nine. Just as often, people have a bad nine and then have a great nine. At the end of the day, they shoot right around their handicap. Many

PGA and LPGA pros have the same problem. They go low one day, and the next day they blow up. They tend to end up shooting the same total score, tournament after tournament. This rule applies for the top-ten golfers the same as it does for the 125th-place golfers. The top golfers just created a higher performance base. I need to convince my mind that I am a scratch golfer.

I read a book, and I apologize that I cannot remember the name, where the author suggested that you should play the up tees until you consistently break par. You can then go back to the next set of tees until you do the same thing. Ultimately, you can play the back tees. The author's idea was to get you comfortable breaking par. Once you get comfortable, you have set a new comfort zone or mean. It would take a very dedicated person to do this, because no one would play with you. I have a group I play with where sometimes we play the up tees. I still had a tough time breaking par. I am not sure I believe in this enough to commit a summer to it. I want to have fun with my friends. It is one reason I play. *Hmmm, do I really want to be a scratch golfer? Maybe I have become comfortable being a five or six.*

Okay, what should I be thinking about?

The target, then the target, and the target again.

For a long time, I felt that if you had one swing thought, that was probably okay. I have since changed my mind. According to Dave Mackenzie, the founder of Golf State of Mind—Alternative Golf Coaching, you shouldn't have any technical swing thoughts. He interviewed twenty-four PGA players, and eighteen of the players said that they have no swing thoughts when they hit the ball. The six players who said they had a swing thought said it was about hitting the ball a couple of inches ahead of the ball. None of them said they had a technical swing thought. Having even a single technical swing thought takes your subconscious out of play.

Your subconscious swing will always outperform your conscious swing. Take driving your car as an example. Your conscious mind really does not focus on anything. Your subconscious mind is controlling the vehicle and, unless you are going somewhere different, your subconscious mind is navigating for you as well. Imagine letting your conscious mind drive the car and telling your body what to do, such as, "Ok, it's time to push your foot on the brake now," or "Now you need to change gears from second to third." You would drive like someone who is just learning to drive a car. Most beginners do not drive very well. The difference between learning to drive a car and playing golf is drivers learn to drive fairly quickly. Why the difference?

Is it that much harder to hit a golf ball? When you are focused on your mechanics, you just do not hit the ball as well. When you are thinking about some technical aspect of your swing, it is the same as thinking about how hard should I hit the gas pedal? The result is that you play more like a beginner. According to Mackenzie, "Better players let their conscious mind go through the pre-shot routine and then they hand it off to their subconscious mind."

Okay, so a pre-shot routine must be the secret sauce to becoming a great golfer. Mackenzie says that having a great pre-shot routine and self-confidence are the keys. He believes that when developing a great pre-shot routine, you should include taking in a deep abdominal breath before you hit. Easy enough, I can spend time to develop a pre-shot routine. I would not even think about boring you with what I do. I diligently go through it with every shot I hit. I think it helps, but I wouldn't say that I see an amazing difference. I do know that the human mind likes having a habit. However, I wonder if it is just the habit or the pre-shot routine? Maybe you should just go hit the ball.

Steve Yellen, in *Simplicity,* shares his belief after thirty-five years of research that the last thing you should think about is the target. He says every sport has its own DNA, and golf's DNA is putting the ball in the hole. Your mind knows this. You don't need to remind it. He says, instead, you should think in the abstract. One of his abstract thoughts is to convince your mind that the ball could go anywhere. He says that if you can get there, your conscious mind has nothing to do, and so it stays out of the way. I have been trying it, and I like it. Once again, time will tell.

In my search, I stumbled across Tathata golf. Tathata golf thought has yet another thought. Their opinion is that if you are properly trained, you don't need a pre-shot routine. You should be able to look at your target, step forward, hit the shot, and then move on. Doing anything else stops time and you lose energy flow. I wonder if Navy Seals do a pre-shot routine before someone is going to kill them. If they want to live, probably not.

YOU ARE WHO YOU SAY YOU ARE

"If you hear a voice within you saying, you are not a painter, then by all means paint and that voice will be silenced."

—VINCENT VAN GOGH

Idiot! You cannot play the game! You stink! Why are you so stupid? Dumbass! These are just some of the things I have either said to myself or that I have heard other people saying about themselves. I have always thought it would be fun to record what some of the people I play with say. My guess is, it would get a lot of hits on YouTube. I have always wondered why I have berated myself to a level that would be considered harassment or downright abuse. I never say such things to my playing partners. I would not ever think such things. When someone hits a bad shot, I usually think, *That was too bad*, or even, *Wow, that was completely unexpected*, or, if a lot of money is involved, I might think, *It is now on me*. But when I hit a bad shot, the negative self-talk begins. Recently, I have gotten rid of most of this. But still.

Psychologist William Purkey came up with the idea that each of us has a whispering self—an inner voice that guides us and helps direct our behavior. The problem, according to Purkey, is that most of us give more weight to negative whispers than to positive ones. Purkey's approach to success revolves around getting people to replace the negative, self-destructive dialogue with positive, reasonable, encouraging dialogue.

A little self-criticism is a good thing. It can be a reality check that spurs you to be a better person. But there is a vast difference between "I need to putt better," which sparks your motivation, and "I'm the worst putter that every walked the earth."

"Excessive self-criticism tends to backfire, because it leads us to focus on our so-called failures instead of the small ways that we could have improved," says psychologist Tamar E. Chansky, PhD, author of *Freeing Yourself from Anxiety*.

Over the long term, studies show, self-trash-talk is associated with higher stress levels and even depression. Maybe this is why most golfers seem so depressed when they are playing.

There are a lot of suggestions about how to control your negative self-talk. The best suggestion I have read is to just ask yourself, *Would you say that to a five year old?* If not, then do not say it to yourself.

My negative self-talk not only happens after a bad shot, but it also happens before I hit a shot. I think the same question would apply. Would I say this to a five-year-old? "Don't hit it into the water." Probably not. You are more likely to say, "Hit it here. That would be a great spot."

There is a great quote from an unknown author that says it all. "Watch your thoughts, for they become words. Watch your words, for they become actions. Watch your actions, for they become habits. Watch your habits, for they become character. Watch your character, for it becomes your destiny."

While the above is great advice, it is something you have heard before. I wonder how many of you accept your habits and do not intentionally try to change them even if you do not like them. They say that we live 95 percent of our lives out of habit. That is something to ponder.

The yips—its own category

Making a change is not easy. I think the best example of how hard it can be to change is when you get the yips. I got the yips five years ago, and I thought my life was going to end. You cannot enjoy playing real golf when you have the yips. Giving three-foot putts is not real golf. I got the yips when I joined a club in Arizona. The groups I play with make you putt everything out. Wow, I was playing real golf. After years of people giving me putts up to three feet and sometimes more, now I must make everything every time I play. This caused me some issues, primarily fear, which caused the yips.

Once you get the yips, you find that everyone who has never had the yips has all kinds of suggestions. People who have had the yips do not say anything. They do not want to disrupt the universe. The non-yippers just cannot understand what is going on. They will tell you to develop a process, just hit the putt and do not worry about it, and so on and so forth. When I practiced, I would make hundred three-foot putts in a row. I would then go out to the course and would be in total fear when I had a one-to-three-foot putt and only make 50 percent of them. That percentage may be high. Four-foot putts and longer were so much easier. It was like some alien was controlling my body.

People felt sorry for me, and I got a lot of suggestions. One was to purposely try to yip when practicing. This tells your mind that you are in control. That helped, but not enough. What I learned is that if you want to get rid of the yips, you need to make a complete change. Your mind must think you are doing something else. This is changing your grip, like to the claw, significantly changing your style of putter, putting with the opposite hand, and so on. I cannot tell you what to change, but I know that you must change.

The same is true for swing changes. You must get some sort of training aid if you want to change. We all think that our conscious mind is controlling what we do. Your conscious mind has very little control over your subconscious mind when it relates to motor motion. It has no idea how to move your body. Its job is providing intention. That is why focusing on the target is the only thing your conscious mind should be doing, or maybe some abstract thought. It depends on who you talk to. Regardless, your conscious mind has no influence on how far you are going to take the club back. Most people have no clue how their swing actually looks. If you watch some of the swings out there, you know that it is true. No one would purposely swing that way. It is proven that your conscious mind thinks you are doing something, and your subconscious mind is making your body do something completely different from what it has always done. Why not, it has not died doing it.

Another theory is that if you really want to change, become someone else. *Hmmm, I like me. I am just not very good at golf.* There is an interesting book called The *Alter-Ego Effect: The Power of Secret Identities to Transform Your Life.* The premise of the book is that if you do not like who you are, then become somebody else. Your mind is just acting out its past experiences. It cannot distinguish between what really happened and what you think really happened. To your mind, the story that you tell yourself is what is true. Hence the phrase, don't let facts get in the way of a good story. So, if you want to become a better golfer, just be someone else, like Jack Nicklaus, Tiger Woods, and so on. Be that person when you are playing golf. Try to think about what you think Jack is thinking about. Or what Tiger is thinking about. Be them. Do you think Jack is afraid to make that putt? Is Tiger afraid of the water or missing hitting a shot? Of course not. In your mind, they've got it all together. So, be them and get it all together.

Is fear part of my mental game? Obviously, but it is a subject that needs some attention.

I NEED TO CONTROL MY FEAR

"Of all the hazards, fear is the worst."

—SAM SNEAD

The most important thing in our lives is our own survival. You can try to deny that you have risen above this basic instinct, but you would just be lying to yourself. We are wired to survive first, procreate second, and then everything else comes next. The survival trigger is fight or flight. All animals have this fight-or-flight trigger, and we are no exception. When the survival mode is triggered, your subconscious takes over. Your heart rate increases, your breath become very shallow, your muscles tense up. Everything is geared to either run away as fast as possible or to attack as fiercely as possible. Okay, this is all interesting, but a reasonably intelligent person would say that there is nothing in golf that should trigger your survival mode unless you have pissed off your playing partners and they are going to kill you with a golf club.

Unfortunately, your survival trigger does not act logically, it acts emotionally. If you are about to do something that causes you any degree of fear or anxiety, your survival mode kicks in. When you experience an event and your reaction is emotionally negative, your subconscious starts to create a wire. Actually, it releases a concoction of chemicals that stimulates your body to act a certain way. The more often you react to that event, the more these chemicals are released. After a while, your body will release these chemicals by just thinking about the situation. Your body does not judge good or bad, it judges whether it survived. If you survived, it believes what happened was good, even if your conscious mind did not believe it was.

The problem is, your conscious mind is very lazy. It only likes to activate itself when the subconscious mind does not have a satisfactory answer and needs help. Your subconscious mind does not need help very often. The subconscious mind creates habits so it can easily manage the world. Remember, it is only trying to survive, not make the world a better place. Trying to change these habits takes energy, and this is not in the best interest of your subconscious, so the battle begins.

Golf creates a lot of emotional fear. All golf experts would tell you that you when you play golf, you need to just accept the results and move on to the next shot. That's great advice, but it's not so easy to do. Golf constantly beats up your psyche, I think more than any other sport. They say that older golfers struggle over short putts much more than a young person. The old person has been reacting negatively to missing short putts for years, therefore increasing his fear.

Let us go through some shots that occur in a round of golf.

I am on the number one tee, and I am looking down the fairway. If I hit it right, I am in the trees, and if I hit it left, I am out of bounds. If I go out of bounds, it is a two-stroke penalty. If I go into the trees, the chance of getting par is small. My goal is to shoot par today. I cannot afford not to miss the fairway. Bam—fear!

I am standing on the fairway, hitting my second shot. There is a deep bunker to the right and water to the left of the hole. I just hit a poor chip shot on the last hole, and I need to make no worse than par. If I miss the green, the chances of me making bogey or worse is high. Bam—fear!

I am standing over a thirty-foot putt that breaks hard to the left. I need to get this close, so I do not have to make a long second putt to avoid three putting. Bam—fear!

I am standing over a two-foot putt. I must make this. No one misses these putts. *Does it break, or should I just hit it hard into the hole?* I hate these putts. Why doesn't someone just give it to me? Bam—fear!

Every shot in golf has a theoretical consequence to it. The key word is theoretical. There is no true consequence to hitting a good shot or bad shot. It is just a shot. However, the consequences of some shots are much more devastating to your score. Like hitting it out of bounds, into the water, or into the junk. Missing a short putt is the most devastating. You cannot get that stroke back. For some reason, hitting what we think is a bad shot makes us think we might be ridiculed (although I have never seen anyone be ridiculed for hitting a bad shot). Now if you have a partner, they may roll their eyes, but ridicule, no. In the past, getting ridiculed could mean getting kicked out of the tribe. Getting kicked out of the tribe meant you die. Missing other shots, like the ball not going as far as you wanted it to or slightly in the wrong direction, may not cost you much, but it is still not what you wanted. The chances are you will try to compensate for these misses. We do not compensate when the other side happens, like the ball unexpectedly going into the hole, a hole in one, chipping in, making a thirty-foot putt, and so on. Hitting a perfect drive or a perfect iron also has a certain amount of pleasure to it. Unfortunately, the number of bad shots to good shots is almost ten to one. Ben Hogan said that he only expected to hit five or six good shots a round. I was just told that when Tiger won the US Open by fifteen shots, he said he only had one perfect shot. These are the best ball strikers the world has ever known. Golf constantly reinforces negatives, which potentially puts you in survival mode for four hours. I think the question to ask is what a bad shot or a good shot is. Most shots are good enough. Maybe it is a game of mediocrity.

In other games where accuracy is a key component to the game, you get to keep trying the same shot over and over again. There is no other game where the playing field changes on every attempt, and the instrument used to play the game has fourteen different options. In bowling, the ball, the lane, the number of pins, and the location of the pins do not change. In basketball, the hoop is the same height for every shot, and the court is the same size. The distance per shot varies, but everything else stays the same. In tennis, the court is the same size, and the racquet is the same for every shot. In baseball, the pitcher is throwing over the same plate, you have the same bat in your hand, and the field is the same. In golf, every shot is different because the terrain changes with every shot. Second, you have fourteen different clubs you could use. Each club reacts slightly differently. Last, you typically have anywhere between thirty seconds to ten minutes (unfortunately) to hit the next shot. This is a lot of time to think about a lot of stuff before you hit your next shot. For most of us, we think about terrible things. Now I am not saying that all sports do not have aspects to them that make them difficult; however, I believe that golf triggers your fight-or-flight mechanism more than any other sport. Bad shots, which are every shot that is not close to perfect, outweigh the good shots by well over 90 percent. There is no doubt that if you let the bad shots get to you, your fear level will continue to grow. Fear adversely affects your game. If you do not believe me, watch someone who has gotten the yips on short putts. The yips are 100 percent caused by fear.

I do not think the fear factor is as prevalent in other sports. All sports have a consequence for screwing up; however, with most sports, you have a chance to do it again immediately. If you are bowling, you are rolling the ball down the same lane again. In baseball, you are trying to hit the ball again. There is a high level of repeatability in other sports. In golf, there is little repeatability. In eighteen holes of golf, the only shot that is the same is a putt of less than six inches. Now you can say that putting is the same because it is the same motion. However, every putt has different distances, different speeds for similar distances, and different breaks, which are not easily detected. Every time you hit your driver, you are looking at something different than the previous hole. The designers purposely design the holes to try and confuse you. Once you hit your drive, you must hit three or more shots before you might hit it again. Not much repeatability.

Unfortunately, I have not read anything that helps me with controlling fear except for changing your physiology, like smiling, breathing deeply, and so on. This tells your subconscious mind that everything is okay. You are safe. Now go hit the shot. Sadly, it takes a fraction of a second for the fear to reappear.

I just need better data.

I NEED BETTER DATA

"The measurement and analysis of golf's numbers will eventually change every element of the game."

—ARCCOS GOLF

I know what my problem is, I just do not have the data. If I knew all of my key data points, I would know what I need to work on. Not everything in my game could be bad.

I need to have goals. Without a measurable goal, how do I know if I am progressing? I have read about elite coaches, and they painstakingly measure everything. Golf pros know their numbers, or their coach does. They say that great companies have a single metric they focus on. All other metrics should support that metric. Only use metrics that work toward the primary goal. In my case, it is being a scratch golfer. Luckily in golf, there is a single great metric that shows your improvement or lack thereof. Your GHIN handicap index. Your GHIN handicap is the average of your best eight scores out of your last twenty and is considered the standard in determining you golfing ability. Now, there are a lot of problems with this index, but it is a consistent measure on where your golf game currently stands.

Every key metric is typically driven by several other metrics that are, in turn, driven by several other metrics. I broke down the key components that drive each metric to ensure that I am focusing on the components that are hindering my progression. This is only important because I do not have unlimited practice time (okay, I do, but most people do not). I need to properly allocate my time to work on weaknesses or to make my strengths even better.

There are a lot of different metrics that you can capture in golf. Fairways hit, greens in regulation, number of putts, driving distance, scrambling percentage, and on and on. Currently, there is a new application that computes your handicap in all phases of the game. They use a concept called strokes gained. I think this is the best approached that has been created to date.

I concluded that there are two primary metrics that drive score. One of these metrics has become very popular on the tours. I am not sure why the other one hasn't. I believe that everything else is a subset of these two.

1. Proximity to the hole—how close the ball is to the hole after you hit the shot to hit the green in regulation.

2. Strokes gained putting (modified calculation)

I also think you should understand your mind handicap because it affects both metrics.

Some of you might be saying that greens in regulation should be included. I think greens in regulation is a substandard metric to proximity to the hole for the following reason.

Proximity to the hole

Proximity to the hole is how close you are to the hole after you hit the shot to hit the green in regulation. The closer you are to the hole, the greater chance you have making par, birdie, or eagle. All positives. The further away you are, the more likely it is that you will make bogey or worse. When Tiger dominated the golf world, his proximity to the hole was around fifteen feet, while the average PGA pro was around twenty-two feet. Does not seem like a lot, but when you look at putting percentages from fifteen feet to twenty-two feet, it is huge.

The reason greens in regulation (GIR) is a substandard metric to proximity to the hole is quite simple. Let's say the pin is tucked in the back left corner. I hit a shot to ten feet, but it is in the fringe. No GIR for me. However, my partner does hit the green, but is sixty feet away. He gets a GIR. Now who has a better chance to make par or better? I would say I do. I would also bet a lot of money that if this happened for eighteen holes, I would win by two to three shots.

Okay, I understand that I could be closer to the hole and have a terrible lie or be in a bunker. However, I think, on average, it is unlikely that if you are hitting it close to the hole, you are in trouble. There is an application that tracks stroked gain ball striking, but it ignores the effects of driving. I decided that you should not separate these because a bad driver of the ball does not mean you cannot score. Look at Michelson and Woods.

Proximity to the hole does combine driving accuracy and ball striking. How far are you from the hole after you hit second shot on par fours, first shot on par threes, and third shot on par fives? If you hit the green in two on a par five, you would still measure how far away you are after you putt. Okay, from here, you can start breaking down this metric into its components. However, you need to be careful that you are tracking the right stuff. I would also suggest, based on the book *With Winning in Mind* that you only track positive results. Focusing on negative stuff is harmful to your mind and your ability to get better. Also, keep it simple. Here is a tracking system.

- For driving: After you hit your drive, determine if you have a reasonable shot at getting the next ball on the green for par fours or if you can put the next ball in a position to easily hit the green on par five. If yes, count that drive. If not, forget about it. Now you can track how many times you had a reasonable chance to hit the green. In the end, that is all that is important.

- For ball striking: You track how close you were to the hole. If you did not have a reasonable chance to get to the green, do not track that because there is nothing to track.

Strokes Gained Putting

Everyone measures how many putts you had. They still talk about it on TV. This metric is not very meaningful. I can hit eighteen greens in regulation, have thirty-six putts, and shoot par. This would be considered a poor putting round. Another person could hit nine greens in regulation and have twenty-eight putts. Wow, twenty-eight putts is great. Would you rather shoot seventy-two or seventy-three? I think the seventy-two is better. The reality is the worse you hit the ball, the lower number of putts you will probably have. The chances of you not being able to get up and down at least one or two times is pretty low.

A better metric is how many strokes are you gaining or losing. Strokes gained putting is calculated it by taking the average number of putts within defined lengths for the entire field and comparing your putts to the average. If you are above average, you gain strokes, and if you are below average, you lose strokes. You need to do this against the field because everyone is playing on the same greens. Unfortunately, there is currently no practical way to capture this information for the everyday golfer. Technology has somewhat solved the problem. There is an app that will measure the length of each of your putts and compare that data with the other golfers who are using the app, plus they may include other statistics that is out there. This application will compute your stroke gained putting and your putting handicap. The problem with this is greens can be significantly different in length. Now I am just getting picky.

This app tracks several metrics. How well you putt, your ability to scramble (pitch and chip), and your ball-striking ability. How close do you hit to the hole? I think it would tell me something about my game. *Hmmm, I should buy it.*

There are a lot of other suggested metrics, but I concluded that most of them indirectly affect the ultimate metric (score). I decided that they are not that useful. Some may be harmful if they focus on negative things, like three-putting and penalty shots. I learned this the hard way. I decided to track the number of three putts I had. My three putts seemed to increase because I was focused on not three putting. Not a positive thought.

Measurement is important. I also know that the only way to truly know where you are struggling is to know the facts. Otherwise, you are just reacting to your latest miss. However, measurement only means something if you have a plan.

A plan sounds like training. That's it, I need to go into training and get out of the instructional mode.

I NEED TO BE TRAINED

"A golfer has to train his swing on the practice tee, then trust it on the course."

—DR. BOB ROTELLA

Training? Only the pros talk about training. We only talk about instructional topics. Is this the core problem? We do not train. We work on instruction. No one ever trained me. I never trained myself. Whose fault is that? Do I need to take responsibility?

I was sitting watching the Golf Channel, a common pastime of mine. I believe that somehow it will magically transform my game. Okay, so while watching some show, Gary McCord and Brandel Chamblee were doing a commercial about a program called Tathata golf. It was a good commercial, convincing, and it does not take much for me to try a golf gimmick. I looked it up on their website and discovered something interesting. Tathata golf combines the concepts of martial arts with golf. *Never heard of that before, but what the heck? I am up for anything that might help.*

Why are martial arts different than golf? First, you need to understand why martial arts was originally created. Someone or some group wanted the ability to defend themselves against a group of attackers. Martial arts are truly about survival. If you wanted to survive, you needed to be able to perform at an elevated level without any thought. You just had to react. Interestingly, martial arts, like golf, has a grading system. You begin as a white belt, then you work your way up to a black belt. Once you become a black belt, there are then various degrees of black belt until you become a master. Currently, it takes three to five years to become a black belt if you spend four hours a week, TRAINING. You might have noticed that training is in all caps. I did that for a reason. This might be the magical answer.

Training is defined as causing someone to develop an ability or a skill, as compared to teaching, which is to show or explain someone how to do something.

There is the problem. I have been taught a lot of different things. I have never been trained. I have heard and seen multiple ideas and concepts about how to play golf. No one has ever said, "Let me train you." Training is converting ideas into a skill or an ability. I have 7,439 different ideas. I need one skill. No one has offered a true training course. I wonder why? Maybe because teaching is more profitable than training. Maybe no one has ever thought about it. I need to learn how to train myself.

I decided to talk to some PGA pros about why the golf industry does not train people like martial arts does. They gave me various excuses, but the biggest one is that people do not want to spend the time to get trained. They have accepted that when someone comes to them and want to hit a spinning back kick, they tell them to keep their head still and their left arm straight. In martial arts, they would say you are not ready to do this. We must start at the beginning. In martial arts, people seem to accept this. Not in golf!!!

Until now, I do not know of a golf training program that has been developed. There are books on drills, and there are some digital programs these days that promise that they will make you into a scratch golfer. I have signed up for some of them, and they turn out to be more instructional. When I was a kid, I was a fairly good swimmer and swam competitively. In swimming, you train. You have a defined schedule of activities you go to and definitive goals for each activity. You did not deviate. You were being trained.

Golf pros have become experts, and it is easier to tell people what you know than to train them how to do it. It is difficult to create a program that trains people to be successful. That would take a significant amount of effort and time. It is much easier to espouse wisdom. I do not believe that every golf training program must be the same, just like there are numerous versions of martial arts. The same could be true of golf, yet there should be some training programs. There is nothing out there that trains you. You can sign up for a golf school. You can go for a week, and then you are good to go. *Probably not.* You can sign up for a group of lessons with your pro. You take a lesson for an hour, and then you leave for a week. You start the entire process over the next week. They all start with the same question. What are you working on, or what is going wrong?

I decided to do some research on how to create a world-class training program. I went to Google and did more than fifty different searches. Everything I found was at such a high level it was totally meaningless. I came to the decision that we have lost the art of training people. I think the only people who really train others are the martial arts and the military, especially at the special operations level.

There did seem to be some basic concepts relating to training:

1. You need to have a good understanding what you are being trained on.

2. You must 100 percent believe in what you are being taught.

3. You must be willing to follow the training plan. No deviations.

4. You must be excited about where the training is going to take you.

Tathata golf says it has created a training program. It is a sixty-day program, and you never hit a golf ball. Did I take it? Now that is a stupid question. It was different, but I failed the number 2 above. I was not 100 percent convinced in what I was being taught. They do several things:

1. They painfully take you through the basic motions of a solid golf swing. You repeat critical basic motions multiple times during the program. The idea is to train a complete golf motion, not just show you what one looks like.

2. They base everything on what the best golfers in the world did and are doing. However, nothing in what they are training is physically difficult to do.

3. The things they train at times seem in conflict with what you have always been told, the bad things you have been told. He makes you understand why these things are misunderstood.

4. They are not about getting into certain positions.

5. They come from a place of creating balance or safety. When you can achieve safety in your swing, you are able to hit it straighter and harder.

6. They bring in a concept of creating pressure throughout the swing. Pressure conflicts with the theory of swinging fast. However, you start to understand that pressure creates more power than swinging fast.

All these concepts come from martial arts. You cannot hit someone hard if your body does not feel safe. There is also a lot of time spent on getting your mind into a different place. It is not about accepting the results; it is about anticipating the wonderful things that are going to happen. It is about cheering for your opponents and playing partners to create better karma. You go through various movements; you repeat these movements and your repeat these movements again. The theory is you are being trained, not taught.

What I found interesting there was no discussion that allowed you to do whatever you want to do. It was impossible to refute what you were being trained on. They do an excellent job of showing why it should not be questioned. Think about it, when you are being trained, you are not in a debate, you are being told what to do. Now you may not agree with what you are being trained in, and at that point, you are not trainable in this method. That is okay, but if you want to achieve greatness, you need to find something you can be trained in.

I loved this concept, and I think it might still be the answer. For some reason, I gave up on the idea and went back into my old habits. Remember, we do not like change; we like our habits. If I do not think I am going to die from doing what I was already doing, why change. I think I need my own personal golf training. Not teacher, but trainer. Where do you find them?

JUST GO HIT THE BALL

"Go play golf. Go to the golf course. Hit the ball. Find the ball. Repeat until the ball is in the hole. Have fun. The end."

—CHUCK HOGAN

It is almost the end of the year, doesn't matter what year, I am still not a scratch golfer. Over forty years, my handicap has gone down, and it has gone up. It has stayed close to a five handicap after my first five years. This year, it has crept up to a seven or an eight. I could use age as a reason, but I refuse to succumb. I decide to stop trying to do things to help improve; I am just going to go out and hit the ball and see what happens.

Before I do, I look again at the book called *Simplicity* by Steven Yellin. He promises a different way to get rid of swing prison. Do you remember swing prison? I have been living in swing prison for over forty years. Thank goodness, I didn't realize it, because I would have been really depressed. I thought I was a free man. I found out that in golf, I am not.

In the book, Yellen talks about figuring out ways to keep your thinking mind, or what he calls your CEO, out of the game. Basically, once the CEO gets involved, he or she stops everything and questions everything. When the CEO is involved, it is like going to the craps table and who knows what is going to happen. The goal is to keep the CEO out. This is done by creating distractions in your mind. He has basic cues to help you do this. It is very similar to singing a song in your head when you are playing. Keep the CEO entertained. Mr. Yellin also says that being specific is not a good thing. Abstraction is better. All this time, I thought being specific was the answer. Now someone comes along and says, "No, you need to be abstract." I'm not even sure what that means.

Simplicity has a different way to look at things. I think one of the most powerful is the idea that before you get ready to hit your shot, completely accept that the shot could go anywhere. The reason is that once you tell yourself the ball could go anywhere, your CEO has nothing to do. Brilliant

This book gave me a good idea about how I should go out and just hit the ball. Maybe I am adding something, and so am I just hitting the ball? Interesting question, but I am going to say yes, it does. Okay, since I now know that the ball could go anywhere and I am 100 percent okay with that, I am set. Just step up and just hit the ball. It sounds so easy. *Hmmm, before taking it on the course, I think I should practice this.*

It's off to the driving range. I must warm up a little bit before I try this radical and possibly game-changing idea. Okay, it is time. I decide to hit five balls. Why five? Who knows, but it seems like a good number. For the first ball, I stand behind the ball and walk up, grip the club, set my feet, and go. Scariest thing I have ever done. Who knows where the ball will go? I watch the ball go straight and long. Now that is interesting. Maybe this does work. I hit balls two, three, and four with the same results. Very exciting. Then I come to number five, and my mind starts asking questions about what I am doing differently, and so on. I think I hit the ball fifty yards to the right of the target. Okay, obviously, this concept doesn't work. I mean, I hit one out of five not very well. Usually, I would have hit two or three. Oh yeah, I also started to think again.

I think just standing up and hitting the ball and watching where it goes so you can hit it again is the only way to truly play and enjoy golf. It is a game where anything can go wrong, and that is something to think about.

REMEMBER I AM JUST HAVING FUN

"Keep your sense of humor. There's enough stress in the rest of your life not to let bad shots ruin a game you're supposed to enjoy."

—AMY ALCOTT

The reason I play golf is because it is fun. I love the challenge of the game. I love that no shot is the same. I can play the same course repeatedly and not get bored. I love the mind games it plays with you. I love having beautiful surroundings and enjoying a nice walk. I love the people I play with.

A lot of people call golf a frustrating game. The game can become frustrating when you lose perspective about why you are playing. It is amazing how one day you can hit beautiful shots and the next day you feel that you have never played the game before. It is interesting to watch how people berate themselves because a little ball does not go where they wanted it to go. I find it fascinating to watch people, including myself, buying new clubs in hopes that it is the answer to getting better. People want to get better, but few want to pay the price to get better. They feel that if they just play more, then magically something will change. It is easy to see why so many people died trying to find the fountain of youth. I have watched so many people, including myself, looking for that one swing tip that will solve all their issues. The snake-oil salespeople keep selling, and we keep buying.

I have come to realize that I fell into a trap of "if I only . . ." I also came to realize that this trap is true with all aspects of my life. I guess maybe golf is life, or life is golf. Not sure which. However, writing this book has helped me realize that I am who I am. I enjoy and love who I am. I cannot do anything more. That does not mean that I should stop trying to get better. However, whether you get better or not, it does not define who you truly are.

I have had the opportunity to play with a lot of golfers and a lot of great people. I have played with people who could go low and people who struggled to get a double bogey. I have not decided if it is the good shots that bring people back or the bad shots that they cannot accept. Regardless, people keep coming back. Most of them seem miserable when they are playing, but they keep coming back.

I will keep coming back as well. I will continue my search to become a scratch golfer. Will I ever achieve it? Who knows? However, it is the journey, not the result, that truly matters in the end.

THE JOURNEY BEGINS AGAIN

It's January first some year in the future. This year is going to be different. I am going to be a scratch golfer.